MW00773404

Praise for *Superhabits*

"A rich blend of social science and ancient wisdom, Andrew Abela's *Superhabits* shows how strengthening our virtues leads to well-being. This beautiful book is a must-read for anyone in pursuit of the better life."

—*Arthur C. Brooks,* Harvard professor and
#1 *New York Times* bestselling author

"Andrew is one of the most principled and thoughtful people I know. *Superhabits* is going to be a classic. It is an eminently useful and readable guide to living well."

—*Patrick Lencioni,* best-selling author of *The Five Dysfunctions of a Team* and *The Six Types of Working Genius*

"This highly engaging and practical book provides sustenance for the soul. Melding wisdom drawn from philosophers, sages, and scientists with page-turning stories of everyday people overcoming extraordinary odds, *Superhabits* is a guidebook for all of us to grow and thrive in fulfilling our life's purpose."

—*Kathleen McLaughlin,* Executive Vice President
and Chief Sustainability Officer, Walmart Inc.,
and President, Walmart Foundation

"Unique in the sea of leadership books, Abela provides a pointed, research-backed view on what actually matters. The superhabits described are exactly what executives need to lead their businesses in this dynamic, digital age."

—*Sarah Elk,* Global Leader, People &
Organization Practice, Bain & Company

"The world is full of advice on how to do more, and too short of advice on how to do better. Andrew Abela's *Superhabits* is a clear roadmap to the latter. It provides concrete tools for linking what we do to why we work — and in the process makes us better leaders, professionals, and — well — people."

— *Tom Monahan,* CEO, Heidrick and Struggles

"*Superhabits* brings the ancient wisdom of the greatest thinkers into an accessible and practical framework for living the good life today. Andrew writes with a crisp and compelling style, and illustrates each of the superhabits with powerful, relevant, and engaging stories. This book will motivate you to examine your life with fresh insights and show you how to grow into your full potential."

— ***Denis Beauséjour,*** former VP Advertising, Procter & Gamble, and author, *The Biggest Idea Ever*

"*Superhabits* by Andrew Abela is an intriguing, original study on the perduring value of virtue as the key to productive and beneficial living."

— ***Robert Luddy,*** CEO, CaptiveAire

"There's a shelf in my library, out of reach of all the others, that contains the books that have shaped my life: because they carry unique personal meaning; because they're written by people I deeply admire; and, sometimes, because they're just really good reads. Andrew's take on 'the unique ingredients for a flourishing life' will have a home on that shelf because it satisfies all three of those criteria. He artfully combines deep research across a broad set of disciplines regarding personal self-governance — history, theology, psychology, management, education (the list goes on) — with engaging vignettes and classic Abela humor to teach us the secrets of living our most fulfilling, happiest lives. 'Thriving' and 'triumphing.' These are our best ambitions; this is a book we need."

— ***Peter Buer,*** founder and CEO, NordLight, LLC

"Andrew Abela is deeply concerned with and motivated by a desire for human flourishing. He is a keen observer of the human condition, and a voracious scholar of the classic wisdom on the topic. Accordingly, he has written a book that both convinces that such human flourishing is possible, and presents a compelling argument that it can be — and how it might be — achieved. In short, this is a book that infuses hope into those who read it sincerely, with a desire to become more fully human and alive."

— ***Frank Hanna,*** CEO, Hanna Capital

"Dr. Abela has done readers an immeasurable good — not merely by providing a captivating and enjoyable read on a well-ordered life, complete with practical blueprints for the development of good habits and virtues — but by rooting this framework in that which is sustainable. When it comes to our pursuit of the good life, many humans have tried (and failed) to formularize that which was optimally codified millennia ago. The superhabits embedded in virtue are unique, indeed, yet as this book so powerfully demonstrates, discoverable for those who try."

— ***David L. Bahnsen,*** Managing Partner, The Bahnsen Group

"In *Superhabits,* Dr. Andrew Abela has prescribed a practical and understandable formula for living better, happier, and more meaningfully based on the teachings about virtue by Thomas Aquinas. He has deftly brought the wisdom of Aquinas into the vernacular of the 21st Century. As such this work will provide all kinds of people with the tools for self-improvement. It is an important contribution to behavioral science."

— ***Francis Rooney,*** former member of the U.S. House of Representatives, former U.S. Ambassador to the Holy See

"If employers help their teams grow in the habits of excellence, it will be good for the company, and even better for employees — setting them up for a lifetime of success and fulfillment, at work and at home. *Superhabits* by Dean Abela is the book that every CEO, entrepreneur, and investor should read."

— ***Tim Busch,*** founder and CEO, Pacific Hospitality Group

"*Superhabits* is a work of deep philosophical wisdom disguised as a self-help book. Through a series of remarkable stories of individuals from our own times, Andrew Abela demonstrates how recovering the ancient virtues is not only the way to transform our own lives for the better but is also key to healing our society as well."

— ***N.S. Lyons,*** author of *The Upheaval* on Substack

"*Superhabits* should be required reading for the C-Suite and anyone aspiring to that role. Andrew guides his readers through the habits needed to succeed as a leader in business and explains how to integrate these same superhabits for a flourishing personal and spiritual life. *Superhabits* should replace every other how-to on business leadership and self-help on your bookshelf."

—*Alyson Barker,* Chief Operating Officer, Biomimetek

"Andrew Abela's book, *Superhabits,* is a unique blend of practical wisdom based on the great thinkers of the last two millennia and guidelines for personal well-being based on current scientific research, with uplifting and entertaining examples. This is a book that everyone — professional and unprofessional, educated and uneducated, ambitious and unambitious, leader and follower — should be sure to read and treasure."

—*Kim Cameron,* Ph.D., William Russell Kelly Professor Emeritus of Management & Organizations, Ross School of Business, and Professor Emeritus of Higher Education, School of Education, University of Michigan

"In *Superhabits,* Andrew Abela makes ancient wisdom new, laying out a comprehensive framework for human flourishing drawn from the work of Thomas Aquinas. Where other self-help books focus on passing fads, *Superhabits* is anchored in timeless virtues and illustrated with practical examples. It truly is an operating system for life."

—*John Coleman,* co-CEO, Sovereign's Capital and author of the *HBR Guide to Crafting Your Purpose*

"At Rooted Pursuits, we believe excellence in life and leadership exists at the intersection of ethics and effectiveness. For this reason, self-mastery is the foundation of our leadership training. Using a MECE (mutually exclusive and collectively exhaustive) approach to virtue, *Superhabits* provides a superior and eminently practical modern blueprint for developing self-mastery and attaining personal and vocational excellence."

—*Jeremy N. Gayed,* CEO, Rooted Pursuits

"An easy read and a timely book. Complaining about a deteriorating culture or the effects of the pandemic on our personal and professional lives does little good. Dr. Abela leads us back to some fundamental truths — basic good habits will make one's life more enjoyable, productive and provide a positive example for our friends, colleagues and acquaintances. This subject can seem daunting, because it is, but this small tome breaks it down into bite sized morsels. Pick one of these morsels and get going on becoming superhabinated."

— ***R. Scott Turicchi,*** CEO, Consensus Cloud Solutions, Inc., and Chair, Board of Governors, Thomas Aquinas College

"In a world increasingly driven by science and technology, the humanities are often ignored. In *Superhabits*, Andrew Abela masterfully resurrects ancient wisdom, teaches it with exceptional storytelling, and brings virtue to life in a profoundly practical and impactful way that our society greatly needs."

— ***David DeWolf,*** President and CEO, Knownwell, founder and former CEO, 3Pillar

"*Superhabits* is an invitation to an ancient path of super-truth, super-insights, and super-power for unleashing a super life. We all want a better world, better businesses, to live a better story — the principles and practices of this book will help that change start with YOU. Much like how 'common sense' is not so common, these virtuous habits are a treasure to be renewed and restored on the path of a life of fulfilling our created purpose!"

— ***Mike Sharrow,*** CEO, C12 Business Forums

"Imagine a 13th century monk putting together a system for a successful and fulfilled life in the 21st century. And such a system has seemingly been lost to modern society. Dr. Abela has helped us all rediscover that system in a way to help us in both life and business."

— ***Denis McFarlane,*** CEO and founder, Infinitive

"In today's world, people seem to be more worried about virtue-signaling than actual virtue. They then wonder why they are unhappy in work and in life. *Superhabits* will help you rediscover the core habits that have been at the center of a purpose driven life for centuries."

— *Jason De Sena Trennert,* Chairman, Strategas

"In the new AI world we are entering, we will all need to step up our game. Good habits will not be good enough. Enter Andrew Abela and *Superhabits*. With his easy style and clear thinking, he has produced an instant classic for success in a world moving ever faster. This book is a must read for everyone who wants to become a better version of themselves as we face the road ahead."

— *Stephen Auth,* Chief Investment Officer, Federated Global Equities, Federated Hermes, and author of *The Missionary of Wall Street* and *Pilgrimage to the Museum*

"Andrew is one of the great thinkers of our day. A wonderfully pragmatic blueprint for cultivating simple, lasting habits to overcome challenges, enhance productivity and deepen personal fulfillment."

— *Christopher Lagan,* President, Congress Asset Management Company

"Replete with practical examples, *Superhabits* provides a playbook for joy in life and efficacy in business. A must read for veteran leaders looking to broaden their impact, and for young professionals seeking both career success and personal fulfillment."

—*A.M. (Toni) Sacconaghi, Jr.,* Managing Director and Senior Research Analyst, US IT Hardware and Electric Vehicles, AB Bernstein

"Virtue learned and daily lived is the way toward order in our lives and intimacy with others. Andrew's penetrating discoveries in this book help us relate to the virtues more intuitively and live them more fully, as we work to grow in effectiveness, joy, and peace."

—*A. Trey Traviesa,* CEO, MGT Consulting

"Most entrepreneurs discover that they do not have all the talents necessary to launch and grow a successful business. If they commit to cultivating Dr. Abela's superhabits in themselves and recruit others who exhibit them, they will marvel at both the tangible and intangible rewards."

—*Myles Harrington,* President and co-founder, Grant Street Group

"Andrew Abela draws from ancient wisdom and modern science to help individuals become 'the best version of themselves.' A master at promoting the virtuous person, Andrew demonstrates what it takes to better yourself in a world beset with false models for self-improvement."

— *Gerry Frigon,* President and Chief Investment Officer, Taylor Frigon Capital Management LLC

"Abela combines scientific research, common sense, and page-turning short stories to establish beyond reasonable doubt what we all know deep down to be true: that a happy medium exists between the 'greed is good' philosophy of Gordon Gekko and the prosperity gospel of televangelists. *Superhabits* proves that the time-tested recipe for prosperity and inner peace is much simpler and more accessible than you thought."

— *Flip Howard,* CEO, Lucid Private Offices

"Mastering leadership in today's global markets demands more than strategy — it requires superhabits. This insightful book reveals the system of superhabits for driving business success on the world stage."

— *Sean Mifsud,* CEO, Latin America and EMEA,
Marcus Evans Group

"At the intersection of many more complicated self-discipline, self-improvement, and happiness fads that have been tried over time and now deluge us on a daily basis sits Andrew Abela's *Superhabits.* It cuts through all of the noise with the simplicity of a centuries-old approach to human flourishing and how to live a better life."

— *Chris Veno,* co-founder and former co-CEO of Trion

"Ancient wisdom comes to modern day life. Abela does the heavy lifting here, making the application of these habits so straightforward for the reader."

— *Gates Garcia,* President and CEO, Pinehill Capital Partners

"A great deal has been written recently about 'the power of habit,' but much of that advice comes up short because it focuses only on the '*how.*' Breaking old habits and building new ones doesn't mean much if you don't know *why* you're making these changes and *what* new habits you should be developing. In *Superhabits,* Andrew Abela makes a compelling case for (re-)anchoring habits and behaviors in a deeper understanding of timeless wisdom, essential values, and humane ethics. Erudite but delightfully readable, *Superhabits* should be read by anyone stuck in the rut of unproductive habits and, even more so, by anyone who wants to live a richer and more flourishing life."

— *Mark D. Nevins,* CEO advisor and coach, president of
Nevins Consulting, and co-author of *What Happens Now?
Reinvent Yourself as a Leader Before Your Business Outruns You.*

SUPERHABITS

ANDREW V. ABELA, PH.D.

SUPER HABITS

The Universal System for a Successful Life

Dean, Busch School of Business
The Catholic University of America

SOPHIA INSTITUTE PRESS
Manchester, New Hampshire

Sophia Institute Press
Box 5284, Manchester, NH 03108
1-800-888-9344
www.SophiaInstitute.com

Sophia Institute Press is a registered trademark of Sophia Institute.

Hardcover ISBN 979-8-88911-340-9

ebook ISBN 979-8-88911-341-6

Library of Congress Control Number: 2024944140

First printing

Dedication

To Kathleen, the love of my life.

CONTENTS

SUPERHABITS

Introduction

AT EXACTLY 1:35 P.M. on May 21, 1950, the Peruvian city of Cusco was shaken by a powerful earthquake. Homes, offices, and churches collapsed. Fortunately, a large proportion of the residents were outdoors watching a soccer match at the time of the quake, or the death toll would have been much worse. Even so, dozens of people died, many more were injured, and entire districts were flattened.

The nearby ancient Inca site of Machu Picchu, however, was barely damaged. Hundreds of years ago, its builders had developed earthquake-proof construction techniques that used large interlocking blocks held together without mortar. This design allowed the blocks to shift slightly during an earthquake and then resettle, instead of breaking and collapsing. Had the modern Cusco builders been aware of these age-old techniques, much of the devastation could have been avoided.

Architects in the San Francisco Bay area and other seismically active locations have since learned from the Inca construction methods, and applied them to develop earthquake-resistant structures. They are designing buildings with interlocking blocks, similar to those of the Inca, though smaller and lighter, and likewise assembling them without using any mortar. This recovery of ancient Inca wisdom allows modern buildings to resist earthquakes, like Machu Picchu has done for five hundred years.

There is another recovery of ancient wisdom going on right now. It promises to have a much more comprehensive impact on all of our lives. It will not simply help us to build better buildings. It will help us to build better selves, better communities, and a better world.

✠ ✠ ✠

Self-improvement can be complicated. One self-help book recommends strengthening your communication skills; another says focus on your empathy; still another your journaling techniques. We're supposed to *Start with Why*, have *Grit*, have *Drive*, have the right *Mindset*, be vulnerable by *Daring Greatly*, be a *Badass*, be *Quiet*, learn to *Think Big*, or *Think Small*, focus on *The ONE Thing*, and practice *The Subtle Art of Not Giving a *****.

You wonder: Are all of these things really important? You have a sense that they might be (except, perhaps, the last one). But, how do they all fit together? How can I put them all into practice? How can I ever *remember* them all?

Have you ever watched a child learn to walk? As I wrote this, our grandson Owen was learning to walk. We watched him as he carefully, intently took each step, concentrating so hard that his tongue was sticking out between his teeth (which was a bit worrisome). He had the muscles, and the balance. But each step was a huge mental effort. He didn't yet have the *habit* of walking. It wasn't yet automatic.

There is a set of mental habits, quite as essential as walking, which can be learned. They are habits for managing our thoughts, our actions, and our feelings. If you learn them, instead of crawling through life, you will be able to walk — and then run.

Consider this. Do you or any of your colleagues struggle with making decisions or getting along with others, or suffer from anxiety? The habits I'm speaking about are precisely the ones needed to handle these issues.

If we fail to learn these habits, we can usually hobble along. But instead of doing things fluidly and effectively, we will have to concentrate hard to take each step, like little Owen. Whether it is making a difficult decision, dealing with a problematic colleague, or responding to an emotional outburst, we'll have our tongues between our teeth. If we fall over, it will hurt. Like the city of Cusco, we may be shaken to the point of calamity.

The good news is that, across multiple fields, ancient habits are now being recovered — just like the Inca building techniques — allowing us to live more successfully and to achieve superb results in our daily lives.

Global consulting firms, researchers at major universities, and advocacy organizations are calling attention to these time-tested ways of living. McKinsey & Company refers to them as "distinct elements of talent." Deloitte describes them as core "capabilities." Both agree that they are essential for improving productivity. America Succeeds, an education-focused non-profit organization, considers them to be "durable skills" and in very high demand. The Search Institute calls them Internal Developmental Assets and has extensive research showing that they help young people grow into "caring, responsible, and productive adults." The field of positive psychology, which has been studying these habits for three decades now, refers to them as "character strengths." Researchers at the Human Flourishing Program at Harvard University have shown their contribution to a better life. The University of Michigan's Center for Positive Organizations has investigated their impact on organizational success. The Optimal Work project has a highly effective coaching platform built on them. Professors at Oxford University and at several universities here in the United States, including my own, are working on helping our students develop them.

But what are these habits, these specific forms of excellence that are so important? Classically, they are called *virtues*. They are far older than Machu Picchu, and the power they contain is incalculable. In fact, as the positive psychology research shows, they are like superpowers: as you develop any one of them, your life becomes calmer, more productive, more joyful, and healthier. And *anyone* can develop them through practice.

One of the best, most complete descriptions of what superhabits can do for us was written by a brilliant thirteenth-century Italian philosopher-monk named Thomas Aquinas, who lived 750 years ago. Nearly forgotten over the succeeding centuries, Aquinas's framework organizes the superhabits and shows how they are central to human life. In this book I will introduce you to his system, and use it to integrate three different and important streams of work. The first is the scientific research I mentioned above, in positive psychology, management, and education. This research provides sound empirical evidence of the extraordinary benefits of each superhabit.

The second stream of work is the contemporary "habits" literature. You're likely familiar with bestselling books like Charles Duhigg's *The Power of Habit*, James Clear's *Atomic Habits,* and Professor B. J. Fogg's *Tiny Habits*. These books show convincingly how small changes can have a big impact in your life, by creating habits. Since superhabits are habits themselves, everything these books say about habits applies to superhabits too. But we'll also see how Aquinas's framework shows *which* habits — from the thousands of possible habits you could imagine — most merit your attention right now and will have the biggest impact on your life.

The third research stream is the "rules" literature, such as Jordan Peterson's immensely popular *12 Rules for Life* (and its sequel *Beyond Order: 12 More Rules for Life*) and Stanford University professor Jeffrey Pfeffer's *7 Rules of Power*. Each of these books condenses extensive empirical research about different parts of life into specific rules, such as "Set your house in perfect order before you criticize the world," or "Get out of your own way."

As a result, you will be able to take the wisdom in the "rules" books and turn it into superhabits that become second nature. Instead of Inca building blocks that resist earthquakes, you will have an integrated system of living that is scientifically proven to enhance dramatically the quality of your life and your impact on others.

My university, Washington, D.C.-based Catholic University of America, and specifically the Busch School of Business where I am the founding and current dean, is on the leading edge of cultivating these superhabits in the lives of our students. Our university's unique combination of expertise in philosophy, history, sociology, psychology, theology, education, and organizational behavior has allowed us to integrate these fields of study into a practical program for our students. Our graduates are in great demand by employers and, as shown by a recent Gallup survey, are outperforming their peers in the different dimensions of human well-being, social, personal, and financial, and have a workforce engagement rate that is double the national average.

My purpose in writing this book is to share what we have learned so that others can benefit from our experience. We'll begin our exploration of the system of superhabits with one simple, but high leveraged, superhabit that prevents us from sabotaging ourselves right at the outset.

#1

Restraint

ON AN UNUSUALLY HOT and windy day in August, 1976, Anne Maguire and her three children set out for their afternoon walk in Belfast, Northern Ireland. The latest addition to their family, six-week-old Andrew, was in a "pram," or stroller. His older brother John, age two, walked beside their mother. Big sister Joanne, eight, was riding her bike. She too was keeping close to mom. Perhaps she felt safer that way. That day, it proved to be a mistake — a deadly one.

It was the height of what were called "The Troubles," the decades-long violence between unionists and nationalists, who were fighting over the status of Northern Ireland. As the Maguires walked uphill along Finaghy Road, they suddenly heard several gunshots. In itself, this was not entirely unusual back then. But then came the sound of a car driving at high speed, and more gunshots, getting closer.

Members of the Provisional Irish Republican Army had hijacked a car and used it in a drive-by shooting of British Army soldiers. Those troops, in an Army Land Rover, were now chasing and firing at the stolen car, which had just turned down the hill that Anne and her children were climbing.

The soldiers were all too accurate. The IRA driver was shot and killed, and the car spun out of control, directly toward the terrified mother and her children. It slammed into them, crushing them against the iron railings on the side of the road. Joanne and baby Andrew were killed instantly. John died in the hospital shortly afterward. Anne survived, badly scarred, both physically and emotionally. In deep anguish, she eventually ended up taking her own life.

The deaths of these three children were just another horror in a horrible time. What happened next, though, was anything but typical. The normal response to the violence was "an eye for an eye." Anne's sister, Mairead Corrigan, took a different approach.

After accompanying her brother-in-law through the excruciating experience of identifying the bodies of his children, she walked into the local Ulster Television Studios station and asked to go on the air. She delivered a heartfelt cry for Restraint on both sides, and an end to the violence. The next day, in response to her broadcast, over a thousand people showed up for a demonstration in support of her message. Several other demonstrations followed, and a peace movement began to form and grow steadily.

The broadcast proved to be a turning point. Though the movement faced numerous challenges — from insults, to violence, to death threats — it practiced Restraint. Ultimately, it made a significant contribution to the historic "Good Friday Agreement" peace treaty of 1998, which finally broke the thirty-year cycle of violence.

Restraint is a habit for dealing with desires, and specifically desires to do unworthy things. Unworthy things are things that drag us down, in both small and large ways. Whether it is an impulse to buy a piece of clothing that we'll never wear, or to curse at someone for cutting us off on the highway — or get revenge for the violent deaths of our sister's little children — these desires, if we give in to them, hold us back from becoming our best selves, and make the world worse.

Research shows that people who have developed the habit of Restraint tend to eat healthier, exercise more often, and avoid excessive use of alcohol. Children with this habit tend to have higher grades, better school attendance, and better standardized test scores — all of which result in higher self-esteem, stronger interpersonal relationships, reduced eating disorders, and overall both short- and long-term happiness and life satisfaction. They also lead to better physical and mental health, fewer substance-abuse problems, and greater financial security. Restraint is like a superpower, which is why it (like all the habits that make up our system) deserves the name "superhabit."

Superhabits have all the benefits of regular habits, and a lot more. Like regular habits, they can be cultivated by practicing them a little bit at a time. Once acquired, they allow you to act much more quickly and easily, even under great emotional strain (consider the Restraint that Mairead Corrigan exercised).

Here's a trivial example of habit formation. I used to hate packing. I got stressed having to remember and organize everything I needed for my journey. Often I ended up tossing a bunch of clothes into a bag, forgetting some things I needed while carrying a lot of stuff I didn't. Eventually, I started practicing the habit of using a packing list. I'd work through it from top to bottom. Now I can pack quickly and easily and without stress. Using a packing list has become a habit for me.

But superhabits are different from simple habits like packing to go on a trip, or brushing your teeth, or wearing your seatbelt. First, they have a broad scope. Packing is a habit with a very narrow scope. It's just about packing. By contrast, Restraint is a superhabit with very wide applicability. Once acquired, it can improve many aspects of your life, from work, to study, to keeping your home organized, to volunteering, and so on.

In addition to having a broad scope, superhabits also have a broad range of positive outcomes. They make you happier and healthier. When I finish packing, I'm glad to be done with the chore. That feeling, though, is temporary, and not very profound. Superhabits, on the other hand, have a lasting effect on your happiness. In fact, as we saw above, there's a lot of scientific evidence that the superhabit of Restraint contributes to both lasting happiness and health.

It makes sense that when we use Restraint in what we eat and drink, we'll feel better. But the health effects of superhabits exist even when there isn't such an obvious connection. For example, a number of experiments have studied the superhabit of Gratitude, of being thankful for good things you have received. They show that as you grow in Gratitude — for example, by keeping a daily Gratitude journal — not only do you become happier, but you also experience a reduction in depression, anxiety, and chronic pain. How does that work? We're actually not sure about the mechanism, yet. But there's clear evidence that it does in fact happen.

I can't emphasize enough that superhabits are acquired just like regular habits — by practice, a little bit at a time. It doesn't matter at what level you begin. Neither genetics nor upbringing determine whether you can acquire any superhabit. All that is required is regular practice.

Consider the case of Dewey, a frustrated teenager. His family had moved around extensively throughout his young life. His dad was often out of work, and there were times when his family didn't have much money. In fact, they struggled to pay the rent. One day, when his dad was away working out of state, Dewey and his mom came home to find a padlock on their front door. They had been evicted.

Dewey fought a lot, and shoplifted a lot. When other kids annoyed him, he would fight with them. When he wanted things that he couldn't afford, he stole them. He often got into trouble. He was suspended from high school for fighting. He was arrested several times for stealing.

His parents' marriage was a mess. Once, they got into a huge argument while they were driving. Dewey's dad was having an affair. Suddenly his mom stopped the car. She stepped out, and walked right onto the highway into the path of oncoming traffic. Dewey jumped out, grabbed her, and pulled her back to the highway shoulder. He probably saved her life.

Sometime later, Dewey was arrested yet again. His mother came to the police station to release him. She was in tears, and begged him to change his life. He decided to do just that.

"I started caring that night," he recalled. "I'll never forget it. I'll never forget going to bed going, 'Of all the s--t my mom has been through and that I have been right there watching and witnessing, now I am compounding it with my dumb-ass decisions.'"

Dewey gave up stealing, and redirected his aggression in more constructive directions: high school wrestling and football. He learned to discipline himself. Through his sports practice, and the encouragement of his coaches, he steadily built up the superhabit of Restraint. He also began meditating, daily.

The Restraint he developed has served him very well. After a brief career in professional football, he went on to have a very successful career as a wrestler, where he picked up the nickname "The Rock." Sound familiar? That's because Dewey was the childhood name of Dwayne Johnson, who went on to become one of the highest-paid movie stars in the world.

All three of his careers — football, wrestling, and movies — are filled with temptations to perform unworthy actions. Johnson has occasionally succumbed. (He once called his *Fast & Furious* co-star Vin Diesel a "candy ass" on Instagram, which he regrets). But generally speaking, the habit of Restraint has kept him from engaging in the sorts of destructive behaviors that could have derailed his entire life. And those difficult teenage years? They are now the subject of an only-slightly-fictionalized NBC sitcom, *Young Rock*.

Anyone can acquire the superhabits. The key is practice. In the case of Restraint, it doesn't seem to matter what you practice restraining — as long as you do it consistently, on a regular basis, whether or you feel like it or not. Researchers have studied many different forms of practices for growing in Restraint, such as regular physical exercise, maintaining posture, tracking food habits, keeping a budget, study discipline, and even speech modification (saying yes or no instead of colloquialisms like yeah or nope). All of them lead to a general improvement in the superhabit of Restraint, not simply an improvement in the task at hand.

In addition to practice, meditation can help increase the super-habit of Restraint, as The Rock discovered himself. We all know intuitively that it is harder to exercise Restraint when we're emotionally worn out. We're more likely to snap at others, or binge eat or drink, when we're drained emotionally. Meditation, it turns out, can compensate for this drain, removing a barrier to practicing Restraint.

Swiss researchers wanted to explore scientifically whether meditation does help compensate for emotional exhaustion. They collected volunteers from a meditation seminar and separated them into three groups. Each group watched a series of short, disgusting videos. For example, one video showed a doctor pulling a parasite out of a patient's neck with tweezers; another showed a dermatologist squeezing a large zit. The purpose was to study how our reactions to emotional exhaustion impact our behavior. The first group was allowed to react naturally to the videos. "Pfui! Gruusig!!" (Swiss German for "Ugh! Gross!!"). The other two groups were told to not show any emotion whatsoever. It turns out that suppressing emotion is exhausting. When the videos were over, the first group felt emotionally normal, while the other two groups were in a state of emotional fatigue. The researchers then had one of the fatigued groups practice meditation. They confirmed that meditation completely overcame the effects of emotional exhaustion — which means you can use it to improve your practice of Restraint.

Regular practice in not giving in to the desire to do something unworthy, whether it is unworthy because it is trivial or because it is harmful — along with meditation — will help you build the super-habit of Restraint. And as you build it, you will become happier and healthier.

That's the first superhabit, for dealing with unworthy desires. Not all desires are unworthy, though. Some are quite admirable: impulses to help other people, to fix things, to solve problems. Should we have a superhabit for managing *worthy* desires?

2

Humility

SHE WAS A STANFORD University dropout who had "a really big idea": to create a small, inexpensive device that would diagnose a range of diseases and physical ailments from a simple blood test, much more cheaply than any existing technology. She raised millions from leading Silicon Valley venture capitalists — and wore a black turtleneck, like the one that Steve Jobs was famous for wearing. Thus far, Elizabeth Holmes looked like she was well on her way to joining the list of startup success stories.

Then something went very, very wrong.

The company she founded, Theranos, invested heavily in research conducted by accomplished scientists. But they couldn't get their technology to work. It could have ended there. The process of entrepreneurship is one of discovery, and when one path proves to be insufficiently fruitful, it can make sense to follow another path. The company could have scaled down its ambitions or pivoted to another direction, as many startups do. Or Theranos could simply have folded. Venture capitalists expect that only one out of ten of their investments will pay off in a big way. Theranos could have been one of the other nine. There would have been no shame in that.

But instead, Holmes' belief in her idea and in her capabilities outstripped reality. She allegedly ignored the scientific evidence, falsified both research and business results, and lied to her board and to the public. She seemed to believe that she could succeed through sheer force of willpower.

She wrote down affirmations about herself and how she should act, things like:

I do everything I say — word for word.

23

I am never a minute late.

I show no excitement....

I am not impulsive.

I do not react.

I am always proactive.

I know the outcome of every encounter.

I do not hesitate.

But this forcefulness had a perverse result. It created "a culture of isolation, secrecy, retaliation and fear" among the employees. Eventually, a suspicious *Wall Street Journal* reporter broke the story. It led to a criminal investigation and, ultimately, a jail sentence for Holmes for fraud.

It is one of the oldest stories in the book — in this case, the book of Proverbs: "Pride goes before destruction, and a haughty spirit before a fall" (Prov. 16:18).

Holmes's desire to come up with a cheap, efficient, multifunctional medical testing device was actually a worthy, admirable one. It can be hard to recognize the line between acting boldly and having a haughty spirit. Humility is the superhabit that makes sure we don't cross that line.

The ancient Stoic philosopher Epictetus wrote, "If you undertake some role beyond your capacity, you both disgrace yourself by taking it and also thereby neglect the role that you were unable to take." Holmes disgraced herself and caused significant harm to many others. She was unable to recognize, with humility, that she had taken on a task that was beyond her abilities — perhaps beyond anyone's technological ability at the time.

Does Humility require downplaying our talents? This is a common misconception. Professor Jeffrey Pfeffer, long-time faculty member at Stanford's Graduate School of Business (GSB), is arguably the world's leading authority on power. He teaches a highly acclaimed GSB Organizational Behavior elective course, OB 377 "The Paths to Power." He has written several books on the topic, including 7 *Rules of Power*, which explores the ambiguity many people feel toward seeking or exercising power. But as Pfeffer says frequently, "If power is to be used for good, more good people need to have power." If you want to change the world for the better, you will need to acquire and exercise power.

Pfeffer's first rule of power is "Get out of your own way." We frequently sabotage our own best efforts by discounting our own abilities, either publicly or just to ourselves. Downplaying or hiding your desire to do great things is a form of getting in your own way.

Pfeffer relates the experience of one of his students, "Christine," who faced an issue at work. A colleague was attempting to advance his career at her expense. Christine had been raised to be "polite [and] deferential," and attempted to use techniques she had learned in a "touchy-feely," sensitivity-training class on strengthening interpersonal relationships to address the challenge. Those techniques didn't work, she explained to Professor Pfeffer, because the guy was just not interested in "building a positive relationship or repairing the interpersonal friction."

Pfeffer recommended that she take an alternative path, and begin thinking of herself and her work more positively — and more accurately. It worked. She solved her immediate issue, and went on to achieve a series of major career accomplishments. Pfeffer observed that sometimes "accomplished, successful people tell their stories in ways that downplay their gifts and accomplishments." Such reticence, whether to others, or to ourselves, is *not* Humility.

There's a problem with the word *humility*. To paraphrase Inigo Montoya's immortal line in *The Princess Bride:* "This word, I do not think it means what you think it means." For many people, words like *humility, meekness, forgiveness,* and even *virtue,* indicate weakness. They connote being submissive and mild, having a low view of yourself, letting others get away with things, being passive. These connotations are false.

Humility is not "touchy-feely." It is a clear-eyed, cold-blooded, accurate assessment of yourself and your abilities. Downplaying your abilities *and* overplaying them are both opposed to Humility. (Indeed most superhabits are the mean between two extremes, too much and not enough. These extremes are bad habits, or vices. More on this in chapter 7 on Orderliness.)

The superhabit of Humility is about managing our desires to do great things within the constraints of reality. The way we do that is by holding and presenting an accurate assessment of ourselves, succumbing neither to an inflated view of our abilities nor to the false humility which Professor Pfeffer's First Law of Power urges us to guard against.

In a sense, what you're doing is trying to look at yourself as an impartial observer would. As British author C.S. Lewis put it: to be able to design the best cathedral in the world, and know it to be the best, and rejoice in the fact, without being any more — or less — glad at having done it than you would be if someone else had done it. It's a tough standard, but a worthy one to pursue.

From an early age, Jason DeSena Trennert had an ambition: to work on Wall Street. He earned an MBA from Wharton. He then worked long hours and put all his energy into succeeding as a trader. But he couldn't pull it off. One evening, at a bar in Hoboken, while Jason was complaining about his lack of success, a colleague and friend told him plainly, "A trading desk is no place for you. You're not tough enough." That hurt. But Jason had the humility to know it was true.

Fortunately, his friend did not stop there. Having slammed one door shut, he pointed the way through another. "You like to write," he noted, "you love macro [macro finance, the study of the relationships between stock market prices and general economic conditions], and you like being in front of customers. You really ought to be a strategist."

It was an accurate assessment of twenty-nine-year-old Jason's abilities and interests. He admitted to himself that "my insecurities led me to choose jobs with the express purpose of impressing other people rather than doing something I might actually like and ... be good at."

Shortly after that conversation, Jason decided to move into a research role. It was at that point that he started to gain traction in his career. He went on to found his own firm, Strategas, which has grown into a leading advisory firm, and is now one of Wall Street's top thought leaders on markets and economic policy. Jason was able to follow his ambition to do great things in the world of finance, while guiding this desire according to an accurate assessment of himself and his situation.

Humility is a superpower. It clearly belongs on our list of superhabits. Extensive research indicates that it is linked to greater optimism, positive growth, decisiveness, comfort with ambiguity, stronger social bonds, less relationship conflict, and lower stress.

Management research suggests that humble CEOs get better results out of their firms. Think about that. Wouldn't you prefer to work for a humble leader rather than for an egomaniac, one who listens to your ideas and concerns instead of brushing you off?

Entrepreneur Kim Landi explains it this way: "Great leaders understand that they are not the best at everything, but rather realize their greatest asset is deciphering valuable information and how to action it quickly. Business owners have to be able to make tough decisions, but they need good reliable facts. Leaders who listen to their teams come out ahead and complete a better execution vs. leaders who only believe their way is always the right way."

The key to the superhabit of Humility is an ongoing effort to know and accept yourself and your abilities. It also helps to have honest friends, like Jason did. And starting early is a good idea, too. W. J. King, in his classic *Unwritten Laws of Business*, wrote, "Many young businesspeople feel that minor chores are beneath their dignity and unworthy of their college training. They expect to prove their true worth in some major, vital enterprise. Actually, the spirit and effectiveness with which you tackle your first humble task will very likely be carefully watched and may affect your entire career."

Growth in Humility happens, like growth in any other habit or superhabit, by making tiny changes and repeating them often. It's helpful to think of the growth in any superhabit as passing through the following four stages of development.

1. *Unconscious Incompetence*

   In this first stage, you're not even aware that you lack the superhabit. You routinely and contentedly do its opposite. In the case of Humility, this would be either pridefulness or false Humility. Elizabeth Holmes, in the Theranos fiasco, seemed to be functioning at this level.

2. *Conscious Incompetence*

   In the second stage, you become aware that you lack the superhabit. You try to correct it, but the force of bad habits is so strong that you frequently fall back into your old ways of doing things. Professor Pfeffer's student Christine began at this stage (though she passed through it quickly).

3. *Conscious Competence*

In this third stage, you are starting to succeed. You begin acting with Humility more often than not. You still have to think about it, though, consciously, every time. Jason Trennert was at this stage. He was sufficiently self-aware to know that he had been making career choices to impress other people; he was willing to do something to change.

A sign that you are moving from the third stage to the fourth is that you act on the superhabit more promptly and more easily. You may even start to enjoy it. It is starting to become part of who you are.

4. *Unconscious Competence*

In the fourth and final stage, you now live this superhabit. You easily, promptly, and joyfully act with Humility, without even having to think about it.

The Positive Psychology Research Group at Virginia Commonwealth University has developed a workbook to help you grow through these stages. It's a crash course with a series of exercises, including recalling and visualizing occasions when you weren't humble; considering cases where others did or did not act with Humility; and exploring why you would want to be more humble. It takes about six hours to complete. It can be spread over several days, and is available for free.

For a quick start, here are three "Humility hacks" that research shows will help you grow in the superhabit of Humility:

1. When you're analyzing a challenging situation, force yourself to think about it from a hypothetical third-person perspective, that is, "How would another

person think about this situation?" This creates some psychological distance, which allows you to become more objective about the situation.

2. Have a "growth mindset" about your intelligence. If you believe that you always have the potential to increase your intelligence (which you do), then you're likely to feel more comfortable admitting that you don't fully understand something; that someone else might understand it better than you do right now; or that you'll understand it better in the future, as you get smarter.

3. Make a critical assessment of the limits of your knowledge on a particular topic. Writing down what you don't know will help your Humility.

After all, as legendary basketball coach John Wooden used to say, "It's what you learn after you know it all that counts."

But is it really that simple? For this, and for all the other superhabits — is it really the case that all we have to do is just keep practicing? Don't I need some significant willpower, at least to get going?

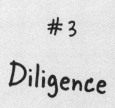

AFTER COMPLETING A BACHELOR of arts degree in philosophy and medieval history, Cara Carleton ("Carly") Sneed headed off to law school. She quickly realized that it was not a good fit for her, and she dropped out after just one semester. Uncertain about what to do next, she took a job as a front desk receptionist at a real estate brokerage in Palo Alto, California. Her responsibilities were to greet visitors, answer the phone, and type documents. Not exactly intellectually stimulating. But she enjoyed the energy and teamwork around her. She threw herself into the work, often arriving early and staying late. She wanted to be good at it and to learn as much as she could.

Her colleagues noticed her enthusiasm. As a result, they started including her in their work. She recalls that they "began to ask me to help them write up proposals, visit and assess property, make cold calls, and participate in strategy sessions about upcoming negotiations. I found I loved the dollars and cents of a deal. It was great fun to figure out how to make the numbers work — for us and for a client. I loved the pragmatic nature of the work. This wasn't academic and it wasn't abstract. You did something and something happened."

Her diligence was rewarded. She soon became a broker herself, and rapidly a very successful one. It turned out that she was only at the beginning of an outstanding business career. After several years as an executive at AT&T, she met her husband Frank Fiorina — and then in an interesting twist of fate, she returned to the same neighborhood where she had her first job as receptionist. Carly Fiorina became CEO of Hewlett-Packard, which had its world headquarters almost literally across the street from that real estate brokerage. She was the first woman ever to become CEO of a Fortune 20 company.

Carly's diligence was the key to her exceptional success. She was obviously hard-working and strong-willed. But interestingly, the superhabit of Diligence is not primarily about hard work or willpower. We often think of Diligence as steady, earnest effort — and indeed that's how some dictionaries define it. It's not primarily about that. At its root, Diligence is about intense study driven by a love of knowing. The French philosopher Simone Weil wrote that willpower "has practically no place in study" because "intelligence can only be led by desire … the joy of learning is as indispensable in study as breathing is in running." The desire to know things is the secret to growing in the superhabit of Diligence.

See what's going on here. The superhabits that help us manage our desires (which include all the ones we've seen so far) are not about using our willpower to force our desires to be what we think they should be, or to force ourselves to do things we don't desire to do. Rather, they are about gently *guiding* our desires into more productive directions and carefully modifying our actions in small and repeated ways. Every little question that Carly asked, every task or project she volunteered to help out with, guided and fueled her desire to learn everything she could about the business of real estate brokerage. Her interest led to her success, which made her become highly valuable to the firm — and eventually to be offered steadily larger opportunities.

This approach to cultivating Diligence by leveraging the desire to know things doesn't just apply to college graduates like Carly. Meet R. G. LeTourneau, who left school at the age of fourteen. In the aftermath of the San Francisco earthquake and fire of 1906, work was hard to come by. He took whatever jobs he could, including working for a time as a woodcutter. He spent all day, every day, chopping wood.

An ad for a correspondence course in the new field of auto mechanics caught his eye, and he ordered the course. At first, he tried studying in the evenings, but he had trouble staying awake. ("I don't know how Abe Lincoln managed to study by firelight, but after a day of oak chopping, I fell asleep," he later recalled). Then he tried getting up at 4:00 a.m. and studying by lantern light until dawn. But he'd get so engrossed in his studies that he'd keep going right through to noon, and not get enough wood cut each day.

He solved the problem by chopping early in the morning, studying from 10:00 a.m. to 2:00 p.m., and then chopping for the rest of the day. He made enough money doing this to buy a small, one-cylinder motorcycle. He put his newly learned skills to work on it, and: "When I could take the motorcycle apart and put it together again in one day, I had a one-man graduation ceremony for myself and gave myself a B.M. degree for Bachelor of Motorcycles."

Over the years, he applied this expertise in a variety of mechanical jobs, at one point becoming a part-owner in an early automobile service center. One job repairing a tractor led to another using the tractor to do grading work leveling land, and then to a grading business. Eventually, he starting designing and building grading and earth moving equipment.

All along, he maintained this desire to figure out what made things work, and how to make them work better. His company's equipment grew bigger and better. They were used in many of the major building projects of their time. Even as chairman of the board of a now vast, global company, R. G. LeTourneau, Inc., you could often still find R. G. at the drawing board with company engineers, on the factory floor, or at the controls of one of his machines.

He even helped win a war. In World War II, his machinery represented over two thirds of all the earth-moving and engineering equipment used by the Allies, and made a significant contribution to the Allied victory.

Diligence is about this desire to know things. Once you learn to channel it, it is very powerful. Studies show that Diligence is associated with better GPA, high school graduation rates, and standardized test scores.

How do you channel the desire to know things? The first and most important thing is to recognize and avoid the ways in which you might be *wasting* this valuable desire. A common unproductive use of our desire to know things is to satisfy that desire with unimportant information. For example, how do you handle the temptation to spend two and a half hours each day on social media, as the average person does today? In LeTourneau's case, he focused on learning about mechanics instead. True, in his time social media hadn't been invented yet — but there were plenty of newspapers and magazines to distract him, and even one of the country's first radio stations, in 1909 in San Francisco.

Is it such a bad idea to relax by looking at unimportant things online? Not necessarily. But do keep reminding yourself: the desire to know things — that you use up as you browse social media — is precious fuel that could be driving your growth in Diligence, and helping you achieve your goals. (Note: when it's time to relax, there's a superhabit for that too, called "Eutrapelia," the habit of playing well, which we'll see in chapter 8.)

A second unproductive use of the desire to know things is trying to learn things that are well beyond your current ability. While it's good to push outside your comfort zone, and to stretch yourself, it's possible to push too far. When your abilities are up to a new challenge, you experience the stimulating, absorbing condition called *flow*, where you feel fully absorbed and energized, even if you're being stretched. But when the challenge goes well beyond your current abilities, you experience anxiety instead. For example, in one of many such studies, music students were tracked while they prepared for a recital. When their skill level matched the piece of music they were performing, they experienced flow; when their skill fell short, they had performance anxiety.

Around the time that LeTourneau was developing his machines, another inventor, Karl Hans Janke, was producing highly original designs for a variety of technological innovations for terrestrial flight, interplanetary flight, and energy generation. None were ever produced. One wonders whether, if Janke had focused his considerable design talents on less grandiose projects, some of them might have actually been built. (In fact, he spent the last four decades of his life in *Krankenhaus Hubertusburg*, a psychiatric institution.)

A third way to waste the priceless desire to know things is to use it up on false or unreliable information. In the final years of the nineteenth century, as Guglielmo Marconi worked furiously in England to discover the mysteries of electricity and radio waves — and to use them for long distance wireless communication — he had some serious competition. Foremost among his competitors was Sir Oliver Lodge, who had an earlier start and was better prepared. Where Marconi was barely in his twenties and had no formal education, Lodge was a respected physicist in his prime who was already being invited to lecture at various royal academies and to demonstrate his experiments.

By all rights, Lodge should have won the race — except that he was distracted by what he believed to be another application of these new discoveries. He became convinced that the same electromagnetic waves that can be used to send messages across great distances could also be used to communicate across the barrier between life and death. He joined the "Ghost Club" and became a member and later president of the Society for Psychical Research. He participated in numerous séances, over a period of many years, and even wrote a book recording alleged conversations that he and his wife had had with their deceased son. Where Marconi's discoveries led to immense practical benefits and consequently great commercial success, Lodge's efforts to communicate with the dead did neither.

Your desires are energy. Your emotions cause motion — they move you forward, and fuel your activity and achievements. The first way to grow in the superhabit of Diligence is to avoid wasting the valuable energy of the desire to know on what is unimportant, or beyond your current capacity — or just downright silly.

Another way to grow in Diligence is to recognize that superhabits tend to be contagious. (This should not be surprising, given that human desire itself seems to be contagious — as my Busch School colleague Professor Luke Burgis shows in his book *Wanting: The Power of Mimetic Desire in Everyday Life*.) You can catch a superhabit, at least to some extent, just by spending time with other people who have that superhabit. When you are with people who are diligent, you are more likely to become diligent yourself. One study found that college students who were randomly assigned roommates who had a history of studying a lot ended up studying more themselves, and achieving higher GPAs, than students whose assigned roommate did not study as much.

We've saved the hardest question for last: What if you just don't care? What if you're in a job where you're *Just. Not. Interested.* in any aspect of your work, and it's not an option to find another job in an area that is more interesting to you? Can you *create* the desire to know things? The good news here is that the answer is an unqualified yes.

Extensive research on encouraging student learning shows that interest in a particular area can be developed, even when you have little or no interest to start with. The same research also shows that interest can be developed at any age, not just when you're young. Importantly, the process of cultivating interest is intrinsically rewarding, satisfying in itself, so that it becomes its own motivation to continue to increase the desire to know things.

How can you create the interest you need to increase your desire to know things and cultivate the superhabit of Diligence? Here are three researched-based ideas to increase your own interest or help others in increasing theirs:

1. *Choice:* Be selective about particular aspects of the subject in which you want to cultivate interest. Let's say that you're studying machine learning. If you can choose which problems you'd like to engage with, and which data sets you'd like to mine, that can help strengthen your interest.

2. *Personalization:* Focus on how what you're learning could be relevant and useful to you. For example, consider how you can use machine learning in your own life and work.

3. *Group work:* Work with others on a project related to the area in which you're trying to develop an interest, where the group is given plenty of latitude on how to solve it. When together you have the freedom to take any approach you like, this can also encourage interest as you explore different approaches.

Helping yourself, and others, to get more interested in something is the key to growing in the superhabit of Diligence. More generally, growing in superhabits means that you are coaxing your desires gently in the direction you want them to go, through little changes repeated over time, rather than trying to force them with your willpower.

Perhaps at this point it seems a little too good to be true. Is it really the case that I don't have to apply much willpower, and just by making small changes, repeated over time, I can develop multiple superpowers that will make me happier, healthier, and more effective? If it's that easy, and effective, how come no one seems to have heard about this before?

#4

Habits vs. Superhabits

HE WAS 1/100TH OF a second short. It was the 1984 Summer Olympics in Los Angeles, CA. Daley Thompson had just completed the 1,500-meter run, the final event in the decathlon — the sport he was born to compete in. His combined performance in the various running, jumping, and throwing events that make up the decathlon had earned him his second Olympic gold medal. But his 1,500-meter time was 1/100th of a second shy of scoring enough points to win back the world decathlon record.

The son of a Nigerian father and Scottish mother, Thompson was raised in London, England. He showed early promise as an athlete. As a teenager, he was a capable sprinter, and had recently tried shot put and high jump. On a whim, he entered the Welsh Open decathlon in 1975 when he was sixteen. He won the event, and also set a new national junior record. Later that year he qualified for the British Olympic team, and in the 1976 Montreal Olympics he finished eighteenth. Two years later he finished second at the European championships. He was then just twenty years old. For the following nine years he would sweep the sport at every level. He didn't lose a single decathlon.

A triathlon combines three sports, or "disciplines," as they're called: swimming, cycling, and running. A pentathlon includes five: fencing, swimming, horse riding, pistol shooting, and running. A heptathlon has seven. Most impressive of all is the decathlon, which consists of ten track and field disciplines. It takes place over two days. Day one includes the 100m, long jump, shot put, high jump, and 400m. Day two has 110m hurdles, discus, pole vault, javelin, and 1500m. Given the wide range of athletic ability required to succeed across such a wide range of events, the winner of the decathlon is traditionally and fittingly dubbed "the World's Greatest Athlete."

Thompson's performance in the decathlon was unequalled. He won three Commonwealth Games titles, two European Championships titles, and two Olympic Gold medals (1980 and 1984).

A year after the LA Olympics, after some questions were raised, officials reviewed the photo finish of his 1,500m Olympic run. They found that his time was actually 1/100th of a second faster than they had previously concluded. He did win the world record after all. He thus became the first athlete ever to hold the European, Commonwealth, World, and Olympics titles in a single event simultaneously. He was truly the World's Greatest Athlete.

How did Thompson achieve all this? He certainly seems to have had a gift for a broad range of track and field sports. He was also immensely competitive. Thompson had a punishing daily regimen, training for eight hours each day (including Christmas Day). He lived and breathed decathlon. You have to be outstanding in all ten disciplines; that's what winning the decathlon takes. Daley's friend Sebastian Coe, himself a four-time Olympic Gold medalist in track and field, said of Daley that "It's not enough to win; he has to mentally destroy his opponent."

Superstars like Daley are rare. It is extremely difficult to achieve what they achieve. This book is about abilities that have a much wider scope than a decathlon — and yet anyone can achieve them. Furthermore, with the "disciplines" of superhabits, beginning is winning; there is no lag. The moment you begin to train for a superhabit, you'll experience your life getting easier, happier, and healthier. You're winning from the start. Mastering the superhabits is like becoming the World's Greatest Athlete of Life.

The "habits books" that I mentioned in the introduction show that small changes, repeated regularly, can have a big impact on your life. Take Stephen Guise, for example. He was frustrated with his inability to get in shape. He just didn't have the willpower to do the exercises necessary. Then he tried one small change — he started with just *one* push-up. Just one! Anyone can do just one push-up. The key was to *make that one push-up a regular habit.* Eventually, one became two, and then more — and finally, a healthy lifestyle with regular workouts. Stephen now writes the Tiny Buddha blog, and has several million followers.

When you make something a habit, by repeating it, you make it easier to do. In a sense, it becomes part of you. Building habits is a very effective way to improve your life.

But if you really want to improve your life quickly, you need to know *which* habits provide the greatest benefits, the highest leverage, to make your life easier, happier, and more effective. This book is about the habits that ancient traditions *and* modern social science agree are *the most important habits* in your life — the superhabits.

You may be wondering: If these superhabits are so valuable, why haven't I heard more about them? A big reason, I think, is that in our society we tend to default to process over content. We're happy to tell people *how* to do something, but hesitant to propose *what* to do, for fear of seeming to be judgmental. As a result, habits books tell us *how* to develop habits, but they don't say much about *which* habits to develop.

Yet consider this: What if you had a recipe that told you how to make the world's best soufflé (the process), but didn't tell you which ingredients (the content) to put in it? What if it told you to preheat the oven to four hundred degrees, coat the bottom and sides of the soufflé dish, melt some ingredients in a separate bowl, blend other ingredients until the mixture is fluffy and holds its peaks, and so on — but it didn't explain that you should use eight ounces of bittersweet chocolate, six eggs, and half a teaspoon of cream of tartar?

It's true that soufflés can be made from a whole host of ingredients, including peaches, cheese, chicken, potatoes, even cauliflower.

So the same process could certainly be applied to different types of content. Still, process alone is not enough. At some point, you need to know which ingredients to put in.

It's the same for habits. While cultivating habits is a powerful force for personal change, it is just as important to choose the *right* habits and to understand how they all fit together. Like a soufflé, human flourishing also has its process *and* its ingredients. We need to know what they are.

It is important to recognize which habits are superhabits, because they are different from regular habits. They are much more fundamental, more broadly applicable, and have a much higher impact on your life than regular habits. The habit of brushing your teeth, for example, just applies to brushing your teeth. The superhabit of Courage — which you might develop, say, on the football field — is applicable to an interview, a presentation, facing an illness, or in countless other challenges.

The impact of superhabits can be truly astounding. We've already seen how the superhabit of Restraint can lead to better physical and mental health, fewer substance abuse problems, and better financial security; how Humility is linked to lower stress, greater happiness, and greater quality of life; and how Diligence is associated with a whole range of positive outcomes. A similar pattern of impressive results is repeated across all the superhabits: the superhabit of Forgiveness, for example, is associated with improved cholesterol levels and blood pressure, as well as lower anxiety, depression and stress; the superhabit of Orderliness leads to greater job performance, academic achievement, and well-being; and the superhabit of Contentment is associated with stronger romantic relationships, better friendships, stronger social connections, and overall greater well-being and happiness. And on and on.

The beauty of all this is that, because superhabits are still habits, you can develop them just like any other habit, by practicing small changes each day. Anyone can grow in any of the superhabits. Anyone can become more orderly, more creative, more courageous, more restrained, more forgiving, or more grateful, and experience all of the heath, wellness, and life success benefits of each. They are truly superpowers, and accessible to anyone, any time.

How does this happen? How does growing in a superhabit make you happier and *healthier*? It's not hard to see how growing in a superhabit like Restraint would make you healthier, because you'd eat better and avoid binge drinking. But Gratitude? Forgiveness? *Humility*? How do they make you happier and healthier? What is going on here?

Here's what I think is happening — and I'll admit up front that this is a controversial claim. Superhabits are not arbitrary strengths chosen from a large range of possible options. No. They are more like wheels on a bus. There is a fixed number of them, and they represent fundamental aspects of our makeup as human beings. Some of them might be a little underinflated right now, or even entirely flat. But you already *have* all of them, even if you didn't know it. You already have the ability to be Courageous, or to practice Restraint, or Forgiveness, or Gratitude. Your task is to figure out which wheels needs inflating — and to start pumping.

Here's another analogy. Superhabits are like underused, or unused, muscles. They're already in your body. You just have to activate them by exercising them. I have lately been practicing an exercise program called Pilates (after its creator, Joseph Pilates). What is distinctive about this method of exercise is that it involves paying very close attention to each exercise, consciously activating a wide range of muscles, and in doing so, strengthening muscles that you don't often use.

There are over six hundred muscles in the human body. Most of us use only a fraction of these. Our bodies try to conserve energy by using only the muscles necessary for each movement. This can lead some, even many, of our other muscles to atrophy. Pilates forces the body to use a broader range of muscles, especially in our core. This gives us better posture, movement, and strength, and generally helps us live better. Likewise, activating and exercising Restraint, Humility, Diligence, and other superhabits, by practicing them in small steps, helps us live better.

Why do I say that superhabits are already within you? I can't prove it biologically. After all, if you dissect a corpse, you won't find Restraint or Gratitude in it. But I can point to two large bodies of evidence that suggest this.

First, consider the extensive research that I have already cited. Can you think of another reason why developing any of the superhabits will make you happier and healthier other than that using these superhabits is how we are supposed to live? Living according to the superhabits is living the way that best fits us. (Whether the superhabits are part of us because we have evolved that way, or because we were designed that way is beyond the scope of this book. It is sufficient for our purposes to notice that the reason these particular superhabits have such an outsized positive impact in our lives is that we are activating potentials that are already within us. We are inflating tires that are already there, strengthening muscles that already exist, not creating something new.)

The second body of evidence is that many different thinkers in many different cultures, throughout history, have identified these same superhabits as critical to living well. Whether it is Plato, Aristotle, or the Stoics, or other writers in ancient Greece or Rome, or in the Islamic Caliphate, or Judaism, or Confucianism, or Christianity, or medieval and Renaissance Europe, the same superhabits appear again and again.

The rest of this book is a review of all the superhabits. As we examine them, you'll figure out which superhabit would be most helpful for you to focus on right now, and how you should start developing it. Small steps will build momentum, first for one superhabit and then for the others. You'll find yourself carving a path through a life that is self-reinforcing, and significantly easier, happier, and healthier.

You will recognize some of the superhabits. You may already be pretty good at some of them; your superhabit "muscles" for some may already be quite firm. But there are almost certainly others that will be quite new to you. Have you ever heard of Gentlefirmness, for example? I doubt it, because I made that word up. The real word is *mansuetude*. But "Gentlefirmness" gives you a better idea of what this superhabit is about: dealing with really strong emotions, like anger.

#5

"Gentlefirmness"

IT WAS PERHAPS THE most famous brawl in basketball history. The November 19, 2004, NBA game between the Indiana Pacers and the Detroit Pistons was in its final minute. Indiana's Ron Artest fouled the Pistons' Ben Wallace, who turned around and shoved Artest, throwing him back some six feet. Several other players got involved. There was more shoving and pushing, but the players were quickly separated and the trouble seemed to be over.

Artest lay his six foot seven body across the scorer's table, attempting to calm himself down. He had been struggling with mental health issues, and was trying to count slowly — a coping mechanism that his therapist had taught him. Suddenly he was hit with a cup of beer that a Pistons fan threw at him. Abandoning his coping mechanism, he leapt off the table into the stands, followed by members of both teams. A general brawl broke out among players and fans. Punches flew. The police were called. The Pacers eventually withdrew to their locker room under a shower of trash raining down from the stands.

The penalties for the "Malice at the Palace," as it became known, were severe. Artest was suspended for the rest of the season, which cost him over $5 million in income. Other players were also suspended, and John Green — the fan who threw the beer at Artest and was right in the middle of the fight — was sentenced to thirty days in jail.

In the early twentieth century, pro basketball games were actually played in cages. Initially, this was because the rules stipulated that if a ball went out of bounds, the first player who got it could throw it back in. The cage kept the ball inbounds so players wouldn't be wrestling for it among the spectators in the stands. The rule was soon changed, but the cage remained for many years more because keeping the ball on the court sped up the game. It also protected the players from the fans. A cage would have been helpful at the Palace that day.

It doesn't take much for anger to boil over into an all-out brawl. Anger is the feeling we get when our desire for things to be the way we think they should be is in some way frustrated. Artest wanted some time to calm himself down. When he didn't get what he wanted, his anger exploded.

In chapter 3 (on Diligence), we saw that desires, like the desire to know things, are sources of energy. These desires should be managed profitably, not wasted.

The desire to have things be the way we think they should be — the desire for things to be right — is also a source of energy. When our desire for things to be right is frustrated, we get angry, and that anger motivates action. Depending on what we desire, this can lead to good things or bad. Sometimes it can motivate action when nothing else could.

The horrific details of the My Lai massacre during the Vietnam War are well known. U.S. troops were ordered to attack the village of Son My because erroneous intelligence indicated that it was occupied solely by enemy combatants. Hundreds of civilians were killed — men, women, children, and babies.

What is less well known is the story of three American soldiers who intervened to put a stop to the murderous rampage.

Warrant officer Hugh Thompson was the pilot of a helicopter providing close air support to the ground troops that day. As he and his crew, Lawrence Colburn and Glenn Andreotta, flew over the village, they started to notice large numbers of dead and wounded civilians. As they crisscrossed the area, the horror of what was happening became apparent. Thompson radioed an accompanying gunship:

"It looks to me like there's an awful lot of unnecessary killing going on down there. Something ain't right about this. There's bodies everywhere.... There's something wrong here."

Shortly after that, they saw, with their own eyes, unarmed civilians being shot by American soldiers. Hugh became enraged. "He was furious," crew member Colburn recalled. Seeing a squad of soldiers chasing civilians, who were running toward a bunker for protection, Thompson said "We're going in." He landed his chopper between the squad and the civilians, who had now reached the bunker and were attempting to take cover within it. Asking his crew to cover him, he approached the lieutenant in charge of the squad. Seething with fury inside, but calm on the outside, he said,

"Hey, listen, hold your fire. I'm going to try to get these people out of the bunker. Just hold your men here."

The response was provocative: "Yeah, we can help you get 'em out of that bunker — with a hand grenade!"

"Just hold your men here. I think I can do better than that," Thompson replied, remaining calm.

He approached the bunker and carefully coaxed the civilians out. There were nine of them in all, two women, five children, and two elderly men. Hugh called in a gunship to evacuate them, and the nine were taken out of harm's way.

Flying back to base, crew member Andreotta noticed movement in a ditch filled with dead bodies. They landed and found a little boy half buried among the corpses, in deep shock but otherwise unwounded. They flew him to a nearby hospital, then returned to base and reported what they had seen. An immediate cease-fire was ordered.

What Thompson had seen, as he and his crew flew over the scene, was not the way he thought things should be. "That was not his idea of being an American soldier," recalled Colburn. The righteous anger provoked by things not being right fueled Thompson's life-saving intervention.

This was not the kind of out-of-control anger that we saw in the Malice at the Palace. Had it been, his intervention would very likely have failed, possibly getting himself and his crew killed by their own side. Instead, it was controlled and deliberate.

There is a superhabit for managing the desire for things to be right, and the anger that arises when they are not. This superhabit directs your anger toward doing good, and it looks like gentleness resting on firmness: a velvet glove over an iron fist. It is the habit that Hugh Thompson displayed so masterfully.

The old word for this virtue is *meekness*. But that word has become confused with weakness, perhaps because the words sound similar — or because passivity in the face of injustice is more often a consequence of weakness than of controlled strength. Another word is *mansuetude*, from the Latin *mansuetudo*, which means mildness or gentleness. It's even more old fashioned and is hardly ever used anymore.

But this is such an important habit that I think it needs an unambiguous name. I propose *Gentlefirmness*. Gentlefirmness is the superhabit for managing your desires for things to be right. It is the habit of mastering your anger and focusing it on fixing the source of your anger; feeling your anger, understanding that it is signaling a problem, and then channeling your anger toward making things right.

Gentlefirmness is *not* a habit of quenching or stifling your anger. Not having enough anger can actually be a problem.

As the slaughter at My Lai spread, Private First Class Paul Meadlo followed his lieutenant's order to fire into a group of women and children. Part way through, he stopped shooting and tried to hand his weapon to another soldier. The other soldier wouldn't take it.

Other soldiers refused to shoot at all. One of these, Harry Stanley, when told to fire on another group of civilians, told his lieutenant,

"I wasn't brought up that way, to be killing no women and children. Ain't going to do it."

When his lieutenant stuck his pistol in Stanley's gut and threatened to kill him if he didn't obey orders, Stanley did the same back. The lieutenant yelled that he wasn't bluffing. Stanley replied he wasn't either.

"We all gonna die here anyway. I just as soon go out right here and now — but I ain't killin' no women and children," he said.

Seeing that he was getting nowhere, the lieutenant turned to Meadlo and gave him a direct order to shoot again. Meadlo, sobbing now, complied.

Anger is complicated. Too little expression of it, frequently as a result of repression, can lead to depression, anxiety, and physical pain — not to mention terrible failures, such as what appears to have happened in Meadlo's case. If Meadlo had experienced the same anger that Stanley did, would he still have obeyed an order that was so clearly, horrifically, wrong?

On the other hand, too much anger, out of control, can cause all kinds of problems in your interactions with others. It is also associated with chronic stress and poorer health, including higher risk of heart disease. (As we've already seen, superhabits can usually be defined as the mean between two extremes).

If you suffer from what are colloquially called "anger management issues" — either too much anger or too little — seek help. There are all kinds of useful resources and techniques for managing anger. Studies suggest that deep breathing, relaxing imagery, meditation, strengthening communication skills, and taking mental breaks all make a big difference. Two well-researched books are

Anger Management for Everyone by Drs. Tafrate and Kassinove, and *Why We Get Mad: How to Use Your Anger for Positive Change*, by Dr. Ryan Martin. (What does *not* seem to work, according to the latest research, are attempts at catharsis like locking yourself inside a room and screaming, or pounding a pillow.)

Brené Brown, in her book *Atlas of the Heart*, summarizes her own extensive research on the topic of anger as follows. Anger often hides other emotions, ones that we don't recognize or don't want to admit. It is nevertheless an effective indicator for catching our attention, and a catalyst for change — but it is not itself the change.

Assuming that you are not dealing with anger management issues, here's a prescription for growing in the superhabit of Gentlefirmness. Whenever you get angry, recognize that your "anger is telling you that there's a problem." See your anger as a signal that there's a mismatch between the way things are and the way you think they should be. Examine your ideas about the way things should be very carefully. The bigger the issue, the more you should invest in understanding whether the problem lies more in the way things are, or in the way you think they should be. Then use your anger as energy to drive change — in the world, or in yourself, or both.

To use your anger effectively and responsibly, you need to be in charge of it. For example, if you receive an email that provokes your anger, wait until you're calmer before responding. If you have an urge to respond immediately to get it off your chest, write your response and save it as a draft. Review it later when you're calmer. Chances are that you'll be glad you didn't send the original version. Then think carefully. Where is the source of the problem here? Where is the mismatch between the situation as I think it should be, and as it is? What is needed to correct it? (Also consider responding to the email by phone, or in person. Emails tend to escalate bad feelings, while direct personal contact, if done calmly, will de-escalate the situation.)

As the apostle Paul wrote to the Ephesians, "Be angry but do not sin" (Eph. 4:26). Anger, like other emotions, is energy that you can use to get things done. So, focus that energy; neither repress it nor let it go in just whatever direction it wants to.

On the thirtieth anniversary of the My Lai massacre, Hugh Thompson and Lawrence Colburn returned to the site of the tragedy. What they experienced there was something they never expected.

#6

Forgiveness

IN MARCH OF 1998, helicopter pilot Hugh Thompson and gunner Lawrence Colburn, whom we met in the previous chapter, returned to Vietnam as distinguished guests at a thirtieth anniversary ceremony commemorating the victims of the My Lai massacre. They were being honored for their heroism in saving lives during that horror.

There were many moving moments over the course of their visit. In one, Thompson and Colburn met two of the women whom they had rescued, Pham Thi Nhung, who was forty years old at the time of the massacre, and Pham Thi Nhanh, who was six. The meeting was bittersweet. Both shared their gratitude for the intervention that had saved their lives. Both remembered who had been lost: Nhung's husband and child had been killed that day, and Nhanh lost her father.

Later, a man in his mid-thirties with a wife and child introduced himself to Thompson and Colburn. He was the boy whom their third crewman, Glenn Andreotta, had retrieved from a ditch, buried under his relatives' corpses. (Andreotta was not with them at the commemoration because he had been killed in action shortly after My Lai.)

But they were completely unprepared for one incident. A woman from among those they had saved came up to Thompson, and asked,

"Why didn't the people who committed these acts come back with you?" Thompson was devastated.

Then she continued, "So we could forgive them."

How is that possible? How, when you have lost parents, siblings, children, friends, when you have been buried under the dead bodies of your family, when the life of your entire village has been wrecked, how could you possibly forgive? And *why* would you?

The survivors of My Lai said that they wanted to put the memory behind them and move on. They were on to something. According to the Mayo Clinic, when you've been harmed, holding on to the psychological pain can make things worse. In a sense, when we don't forgive, the violation of our sense of what is right grows toxic within us.

Forgiving others is freeing. Novelist Matthew Dicks writes, "When you can find a way to forgive the negative person who plagues your thoughts and feelings, you can find true freedom." Years after the "Malice at the Palace" incident, Ron Artest decided to reach out to John Green in a gesture of forgiveness. Green was the fan who threw a cup of beer at Artest and escalated the Malice to its epic proportions. They have since become good friends.

Forgiveness is a companion superhabit to Gentlefirmness. It helps us manage our desire for things to be the way we think they should be, the desire for things to be right. Where Gentlefirmness is the habit of directing your anger toward making things right, Forgiveness is the habit of moderating your response — whether it be hatred, retaliation, or punishment — toward what caused the anger in the first place. Gentlefirmness is the superhabit you call on in the moment, when you perceive that things aren't right; Forgiveness is the superhabit you employ afterward, to deal with the fallout. You can't go back and change what happened, but you can help heal the consequences.

Forgiveness is truly a superpower. It is associated with both psychological and physical benefits. Studies show that acting with Forgiveness is associated with lower levels of anxiety, depression, and stress, and also improved cholesterol levels, sleep, and blood pressure. Forgiveness therapy is even being used to help treat cancer.

It can be hard to forgive. When former New York Giants baseball player Fred Snodgrass died, at age eighty-six, his *New York Times* obituary headline highlighted that he lost the World Series for the Giants by dropping a fly ball — more than sixty years earlier! (The New York Giants baseball team, not to be confused with the New York Giants football team, played in New York from 1885 to 1957, when they moved to San Francisco and became the San Francisco Giants.) Snodgrass went on to become a successful businessman and banker, three-term city councilor, and mayor of his town. Yet that dropped fly ball is what people remember. Come on, New York — isn't it time to forgive him?!

Studies suggest that individuals can learn to be more forgiving if they practice empathy, self-reflection, and letting go of expectations. Studies on forgiveness therapy found that uncovering one's negative feelings, deciding to forgive, working toward understanding the offending person, and discovering empathy and compassion for him or her helped alleviate symptoms of post-traumatic stress disorder, anxiety, and depression. Two good resources here are Dr. Fred Luskin's book *Forgive for Good* and Dr. Everett Worthington's free workbook *The Path to Forgiveness*.

Scholars at the Harvard Human Flourishing Program consider forgiveness to be so important that it ought to be treated as a public health issue. One survey concluded that almost two-thirds of Americans felt like they need more forgiveness in their lives. Forgiveness also has an important role to play in organizations. Research shows, for example, that employees forgiving each other leads to greater job satisfaction, higher work engagement, and lower burnout.

Forgiveness is also necessary for effective leadership.

On Friday, February 9, 2001, in Honolulu Harbor, it was a pleasant seventy-five degrees, though somewhat cloudier than usual. The 190-foot Japanese ship *Ehime Maru* pulled out from the harbor at noon, with her full complement of twenty crew members along with thirteen high school students and their two teachers. The boat served as a school ship for students interested in maritime careers, and was heading out to sea for some on-board training. It would never return.

At precisely 1:43 p.m., less than two hours after leaving Honolulu, the ship was struck by a submarine. At 360 feet long, almost twice the size of the *Ehime Maru*, the nuclear attack submarine *USS Greenville* was in the area for a brief public relations mission, demonstrating the vessel's capabilities to a number of distinguished guests. Her captain, Commander Scott Waddle, had just led the sub through various complex maneuvers under water, wowing the visitors. For his grand finale, he ordered a rapid dive and then an emergency ballast blow. Pressurized air was injected into the ballast tanks, which caused a swift ascent to the surface.

Once a ballast blow occurs, nothing can stop a submarine's rise. The *Greenville* surfaced underneath the school ship and tore its stern off. Within ten minutes, the Japanese ship sunk. Its life rafts deployed automatically, and many of the crew and students were able to board them. However, she went down so quickly that three crew members, four students, and both teachers could not get out in time, and drowned.

How did this happen? The *Greenville* consistently received above average and higher ratings, and had won several awards under Commander Waddle, who "was an engaged and personable leader." His crew admired him and respected his technical proficiency, and they said that his presence in the control room always gave an added sense of security to those on watch.

The Court of Inquiry Report on the tragedy concluded that the cause of the collision was a "series and combination of individual negligence(s)." These included Commander Waddle's "disregard of standard submarine operating procedures and his own Standing Orders" and the "failure of the ship's contact management team [who are responsible for identifying other vessels in the area, particularly prior to surfacing] to work together and pass information to each other." One such negligence: a video monitor designed to bring sonar updates to the control room was known to be broken, but no arrangements had been made to ensure that the necessary information would be communicated regularly by other means. Another example: the required 360-degree periscope sweep prior to diving was rushed and incomplete, and, in the hazy conditions, entirely missed seeing the white hull of the *Ehime Maru*.

Reading through the report, one has the impression of a captain who is overly confident, and preoccupied with impressing his distinguished guests. Indeed, he is described as "self-confident in his own abilities and quick to take advantage of opportunities to make his command, the Navy, and himself look good."

This leadership pattern is all too familiar. It is one that management guru Jim Collins calls the "genius with a thousand helpers." It describes a type of leader who has a high opinion of his abilities and reserves the important decisions to himself, tasking his "helpers" merely with implementation. The problem with this approach is that it does not develop subordinates' own decision-making abilities or initiative very well. Indeed, at one point, Rear Admiral Konetzni, then commander of the submarine force in the Pacific, had noted to Commander Waddle that he should be wary of his hands-on management style and delegate more, to "give his crew the opportunity to grow."

This problematic — and in the *Greenville* case fatal — style of leadership is at least partly, it seems to me, a result of a perceived lack of forgiveness toward subordinates. When leaders have high opinions of their own abilities, they have a clear picture in their minds of what the right order of things is, and they expect their subordinates to follow their direction and keep to that picture. Penalties for subordinates who deviate from the picture can be high — so they do exactly as they're told.

On the other hand, leaders who are seen to be forgiving are more likely to receive input and initiative from their subordinates, because they are confident that their supervisors will tolerate failure. Research provides support for this hypothesis. A recent study with respondents from six hundred corporations concluded that when leaders are more forgiving, employees are more innovative, which in turn improves organizational performance.

To be clear, chains of command are important. You don't want people innovating in the middle of complex nuclear submarine maneuvers. But you do want them to show initiative, and feel free to communicate concerns promptly. On the *Greenville*, sonar readings — which are essential for getting a clear picture of what is happening on the surface — were obscured because of the high speed and sudden turns ordered by the captain. Neither the sonar supervisor nor the officer on deck raised this as an issue, even when their estimates were self-evidently wrong: they showed, for example, that one large ship nearby was moving at an impossible ninety-nine knots — 114 miles per hour! If they had raised these concerns, and if the captain had waited until clearer sonar readings were forthcoming, the tragedy would have been avoided. The superhabit of Forgiveness might have saved lives.

As we saw in the introduction, *superhabit* is really another word for virtue. Does this mean that superhabits are just about morality? Virtues are indeed about morality, but more broadly, they are about human excellence. Moral excellence, yes, but also practical excellence more generally. It is important to distinguish virtues from values. Values are "talking the talk." Virtues are "walking the walk." There is no doubt that the captain and crew of the *Greenville* valued safety and human life. But that did not save the lives of those teachers and school children. What was needed was practical excellence. In a sense, virtues are values turned into habits. It's one thing to value initiative among your crew, or staff. It's another thing entirely to be in the habit of forgiving them when necessary, so that they won't shy away from showing initiative.

A couple of years before the *Greenville* tragedy, another U.S. Navy captain, Michael Abrashoff, was taking command of the five hundred–foot destroyer *USS Benfold*. The morale and performance of the ship's crew were abysmal as a result of their previous captain's strict "command-and-control" leadership style. He was another "genius with a thousand helpers" — though perhaps not such a genius, and he certainly didn't get much help.

Abrashoff decided to take a different approach.

"In the beginning, people kept asking my permission to do things. Eventually, I told the crew, 'It's your ship. You're responsible for it. Make a decision and see what happens.'"

Isn't that risky? What if his crew made serious mistakes?

"I chose my line in the sand. Whenever the consequences of a decision had the potential to kill or injure someone, waste tax-payers' money, or damage the ship, I had to be consulted. Short of those contingencies, the crew was authorized to make their own decisions. Even if the decisions were wrong, I would stand by them. Hopefully, they would learn from their mistakes."

Abrashoff was giving a clear message of forgiveness: try things, and if something doesn't work, you won't get in trouble. He concluded that "the more responsibility they were given, the more they learned.... The command-and-control approach is far from the most efficient way to tap people's intelligence and skills. To the contrary, I found that the more control I gave up, the more command I got."

Leaders who are forgiving get more and better effort out of their people. Like the other superhabits, Forgiveness is good for our health and happiness, and it helps our organizations flourish.

We have looked at superhabits for managing our desires to do things, to know things, and to have things be the way we think they ought to be. Channeling those desires gives us the energy to accomplish what we want and need to accomplish, without having to draw down our willpower constantly.

But what if I have no desire *at all* to do what I need to do? What if I *really* don't feel like doing it? Is there a superhabit for that?

#7

Orderliness

It was 2:00 a.m. Aliman Sears lay awake in his bed, in anguish. Aliman is the co-founder and chief operating officer of a not-for-profit psychiatric social work agency, Community Empowerment Resources (CER). His agency was doing well. In the previous two years, case workers from CER had received state-wide recognition for providing exemplary care.

But Aliman was overwhelmed. He knew that over one thousand emails waited for his attention in his inbox. He was so inundated with work that his staff routinely expected that he would forget things — and so they were lackadaisical about doing what he asked them to do.

Something had to change. Aliman knew he had to figure out how to get himself organized. He realized that if he could gather together in one place all the things that required his attention, and then sort through them to decide what to do with each one, his life would be less stressful. He embarked on a journey that ultimately led him to adopt David Allen's Getting Things Done (GTD) system, a five-step process for getting organized.

Step one in GTD is "capture": collect everything that needs your attention. This took Aliman a whole month, as he worked through five separate, towering stacks of material. Steps two to five ran more quickly: clarify what to do with each item; organize each item by entering it into a to-do list, project file, or calendar; reflect on what you have gathered, to make sure that you are working on the right things; and engage with the tasks you have identified — that is, do the work.

Aliman's adoption of GTD turned his life around. His email inbox reaches zero at least once a day. His staff know that he'll always follow up, so they pay attention to what he asks for. And he sleeps better: no more 2:00 a.m. wake-up calls from his frantic subconscious mind.

Can it really be that easy to get organized? Sometimes. Much depends on your personality type. The Myers-Briggs Type Indicator (MBTI) categorizes people along various personality dimensions, and the relevant dimension here is your preference for how you engage with the outside world. On one end of this dimension are the "judgers," who like to be in control and make decisions. They tend to like structure. On the other end are "perceivers," who prefer to experience the outside world rather than control it; they would rather have flexibility.

If your preferences lean strongly in the direction of judging, then adopting a personal productivity system like GTD will probably be self-reinforcing. Chances are it will satisfy your preference for structure. Your life will improve and you'll stick with it. If you have a strong perceiver preference, though, words like "organization" and "structure" might give you a sick feeling in your stomach. You can still get organized, but your approach might look very different from GTD. Most people's preferences lie somewhere in the middle. No matter what, you should try to find an approach that works for your particular personality type.

Even if you have to invent one of your own.

As a child, Ryder Carroll struggled with bad grades, impatient teachers, and frustrated tutors. He was diagnosed with attention deficit disorder (ADD) — but in the 1980s, when he grew up, there wasn't much help available for him. He tried to concentrate on what he was supposed to do next, but he simply couldn't focus. His poor results led him to develop a deep sense of self-doubt, which only worsened the situation.

He started experimenting with ways of keeping track of things and staying organized — ways that would fit with how his mind worked. A formal system like GTD would not have suited Ryder. His mind just did not process stuff in that way. "Through trial and *a lot* of error," he wrote later, "I gradually pieced together a system that worked." He developed an approach that was "a cross between a planner, diary, notebook, to-do list, and sketchbook," all combined in a single paper notebook. He found the method worked for his unique personality. He became more focused, and started to get more done, and done well.

He continued to develop his system over several years, as he completed his schooling and through his early career as a web designer. He shared his system with a friend, who was impressed, and word about it spread. Soon he was being asked by others to explain it to them. Encouraged by this enthusiasm, he formalized and streamlined his system further, and then created a website, with videos and tutorials to explain it. It was featured on several major websites and in *Fast Company* magazine. Within a few years, the Bullet Journal method had become a global movement, with millions of people using it to bring more order into their lives.

Perhaps the Bullet Journal method would work for you. Or maybe you should keep looking for something else. Either way, there's strong evidence that getting in the habit of being deliberate about how to sequence your activity will make your life better.

Orderliness is the superhabit for keeping order in your life. It is the superhabit for getting work done by figuring out in what sequence to do things, and then doing them. A critical aspect of Orderliness is time management, and a recent meta-analysis of 158 separate research studies found that time management improves job performance, academic achievement, and well-being. Interestingly, the improvement was stronger for well-being than for performance — and even in cases where time management had no effect on performance at all, it still had a positive effect on well-being. Life is just better when you don't have to wake up at 2:00 a.m. worrying about whether you've forgotten something important.

Perhaps best of all, Orderliness helps answer the question "What if I just don't feel like doing anything at all?" — although the answer might not be quite the one you would expect. After all, unless you're clinically depressed, it's almost never the case that you really don't feel like doing *anything*. Usually, when you don't feel like doing anything, that really just means you don't feel like doing what you *should* be doing. Growing in the habit of Orderliness means channeling your "desire to do something" toward the thing you most need to do.

Orderliness in your activities is supported by order in your surroundings. When your surroundings are organized, your brain doesn't have to work as hard to find things. Disorganized environments, on the other hand, cause stress. More generally, when combined with hard work and self-control, Orderliness is a good predictor of superior academic performance, work performance, physical health, marital stability, and well-being. It is also associated with lower levels of stress and a higher quality of life in both children and adults. Orderliness can even make you more creative (but we'll save that for later when we talk about the superhabit of Creativity).

Like Humility, and most other superhabits, Orderliness is the mean between two extremes. In this case, the extremes are too little and too much structure. Too little structure is the vice of disorderliness — the bad habit of going through life doing whatever thing you feel like doing next, without some kind of organization or plan. Back in my college days, when there was something I needed to do, I would usually wait until I felt like doing it. Guess what? Most of the time, that feeling never came, which meant either lots of last-minute scrambles before deadlines, or worse, things not getting done at all. It was stressful. Too little order in your life causes a lack of both peace and productivity.

But too much structure is also a problem. How much is too much structure? That's a complicated question. Professor Joseph Reagle, in his book *Hacking Life*, describes the extremes to which people he calls "life hackers" will go to organize their lives. His exemplar is Tynan (that's his full name), who describes himself as "a minimalist nomad" who "has spent his life exploring the outer reaches of human experience and making them accessible to everyone." According to Reagle, each morning, as Tynan's "smart phone wakes him, his curtain opens automatically, and as he brushes his teeth, his agenda for the day is displayed on the forty-inch LCD embedded within the mirror. His home secures, vacuums, heats, and cools itself."

Reagle argues that life hackers like Tynan have a vision of organization that is so tightly confined to a particular set of goals that they ignore other important aspects of life. I don't know Tynan, so I cannot say if this is true of him. I do like that Tynan's book, *Superhuman by Habit*, promotes the idea that having good habits reduces your reliance on willpower for getting things done — he's exactly right about this. But the vice of obsessiveness, or too much structure, can arise when you are hyper focused on too narrow a set of goals.

Theologian Hans von Balthasar writes disparagingly of "appointment books in which every moment has been sold in advance." As we'll see in the next chapter on Eutrapelia (the habit of playing well), there needs to be some room for leisure in our lives, for doing things just for their own sake rather than to achieve yet another goal. Otherwise, our minds will never get any rest. When the amount of structure in our lives gets in the way of real leisure, that's too much.

So how do we become more orderly, without going to extremes? There are over fifty thousand books related to time management on

Amazon.com. It's impossible to summarize them all. The main points are that there are many, many ways to become more orderly; some fit better with certain types of personalities than others; if you've tried to get organized before, and failed, it might be because you used a technique that wasn't a good fit with your personality preferences; and, most importantly, it's worth trying again.

Here's what not to do: multitasking. Research shows conclusively that multitasking is not productive. Even when you think you're doing several things at once, you aren't — your brain is just switching from one task to another. Since there are significant costs to switching, it's more efficient to complete one thing and then move to another.

External interruptions are even worse. Not only do they tend to slow you down, but they also cause stress. Try to set aside blocks of time to do a single piece of work, and protect yourself as much as possible from being interrupted. (Cal Newport's excellent book *Deep Work* is all about how to do this.)

Next, do the following: set some goals; make a list of the tasks you need to do to accomplish each goal; and then prioritize each task. Also, reward yourself consistently after completing a task. These things have all been demonstrated to improve organizational skills.

If your Myers-Briggs personality type is "judging" (i.e., having a preference for structure and control) consider the "Getting Things Done (GTD)" system if you incline toward big picture thinking, or Bullet Journaling if you're more detail oriented. If your type is "perceiving" (a preference for flexibility), consider the following.

Molly Owens is CEO of Truity, a company she founded to offer low-priced but high quality personality assessments. A favorite piece of advice of hers is one that she received from a professor in graduate school: "You don't go to the grocery store with a list of what you don't want." So know what you want out of an organizing system, and choose or develop one that suits your needs.

For example, Molly offers the following advice for people who want more flexibility: do make lists of the important things you need to do, but tackle them in any order; do keep focused by blocking your time, but set a timer so that you only work for twenty-five minutes at a stretch — then take a break (this is called the "pomodoro technique" because its inventor used a tomato-shaped timer; *pomodoro* is Italian for tomato); interruptions can be particularly disruptive for perceivers, so try really hard to avoid them (it's hard to regain focus after an interruption); and get help with staying accountable by sharing your aspirations with a friend or colleague, to whom you can report back.

If you have trouble staying focused, consider the Optimal Work online app and its "Golden Hour" approach. The Golden Hour is a period of highly concentrated work. It can be an hour, or more, or less — your choice. The app guides you through gathering everything you'll need for this period, from deciding what kind of ideals you'd like to practice during this period, to dividing up the work that you want to accomplish during the period into discrete steps, to spending sixty seconds of deep breathing prior to beginning the Golden Hour. I have found that I am often more productive in a single Golden Hour than in two hours of less structured time.

Finally, if you already have a system that works for you — but you would like to kick it up a couple of notches — consider the following ideas that author Kevin Kruse gathered from interviewing two hundred ultra-productive people. He interviewed billionaires, Olympians, successful entrepreneurs, and other super-achievers to ask them what their number one productivity tip was. I've adopted the following three and can affirm that they are hugely helpful:

1. "Focus only on one thing. Ultra-productive people know their Most Important Task (MIT) and work on it for one to two hours each morning, *without interruptions*" (That's how I wrote this book while also running a business school, maintaining a consulting practice, and trying to be a good husband to my wife and father to six children. In fact, I tried to do a Golden Hour of writing, first thing each day, every day.)

2. "Touch things only once. How many times have you opened a piece of regular mail — a bill perhaps — and then put it down only to deal with it again later? How often do you read an email, and then close it and leave it in your inbox to deal with later? Highly successful people try to 'touch it once.' If it takes less than five or ten minutes — whatever it is — they'll deal with it right then and there." (This is very important. Implementing this strategy allows me to get to email zero, if not once a day as Aliman Sears does, at least once a week.)

3. "Don't use to-do lists.... Instead schedule everything on your calendar." (Although I do have a to-do list, I use "time blocking" to make sure that each task on my list is scheduled for a specific time and duration on my calendar. What I love about time blocking is that I don't have to worry about whether I have enough time to do all the things on my to-do list, because they're already scheduled in my calendar. It also reduces my availability for meetings, and it helps me say no to requests when I'm already too busy. Most to-do list management apps integrate with your calendar, to allow you to do this. For several years I used GQueues,

which integrates well with Google Calendar. Recently
I switched to Sunsama; it goes beyond just time blocking to really help you plan your day.)

Orderliness is the superhabit that navigates between the chaos of too
little order and the obsessiveness of too much. It is the habit for dealing with the desire for what to do next.

But what if what you want to do next is just to have fun? There's
even a superhabit for that too. It makes our leisure time more enjoyable — and usually more frequent. It can also have life-changing
consequences, especially for those of us who have workaholic
tendencies.

#8

Eutrapelia

LATE ONE AFTERNOON, THEODORE Edward Hook, early nineteenth-century London's biggest practical joker, was walking the streets of a well-to-do part of the city with a close friend of his. As they passed one particularly luxurious home, they caught the aroma of a delicious dinner about to be served. His colleague wished out loud that he could join that dinner party. Inspired, Hook bet his friend that he could get himself invited.

He promptly walked up the steps to the front door of the house, knocked, and was admitted by a servant, who, assuming he was a guest, showed him to where a large party were gathering for drinks before dinner. Hook right away engaged a group of the guests, and had them captivated by his amusing anecdotes before the dinner party host noticed the intruder. Our hero continued his entertaining chatter until the majority of the dinner guests were gathered around him. The host was finally was able to interrupt, and the conversation went something like this:

Host: "I beg your pardon, sir, but your name, sir — I did not quite catch it — servants are so useless — and I am really a little at a loss."

Hook: "Don't apologize, I beg. Smith — my name is Smith — and as you justly observe, servants are always making some stupid blunder or another; I remember a remarkable instance ... " — and at this point, he launched into a long and hilarious anecdote about a bumbling servant.

Once that anecdote was over, the host replied that he actually didn't think it was a problem with the servants, because he "had not anticipated the pleasure of Mr. Smith's company at dinner this evening."

Hook's response was a genius stroke of improvisation, deliberately misunderstanding the point:

"No, I dare say not — you said *four* o'clock in your note, I know, and it is now more than an hour past that, so I could see how you would assume that I wasn't coming. But the fact is, I have been detained in the City — as I was about to explain when — "

"Wait a minute!" interrupts the host, "Who do you think I am?"

Hook couldn't possibly know his host's name, having picked this house at random. But once again, improvisation came to the rescue.

"You? why Mr. Thompson, of course," making up a name "an old friend of my father's. I have not had the pleasure, indeed, of meeting you before, but having received your kind invitation yesterday, on my arrival from Liverpool, here I am! I am only afraid that I have kept you waiting."

"No, no! not at all," replies the polite host. "But permit me to observe, my dear sir, my name is not exactly Thompson. It is Jones...."

And now, the calculated gamble:

"Jones! — why surely I cannot have — yes, I must — Good Heavens! I see it all! My *dear* sir, what an unfortunate blunder — I'm in the *wrong house* — what must you think of such an intrusion! — I am really at a loss for words in which to apologize — you must allow me to leave immediately..."

Which pays off:

"Pray don't think of leaving," says the hospitable, if rather gullible, host, "dinner at your friend's must be almost over now, since it was supposed to start at four o'clock, and I am only too happy to offer you a seat at my table..."

There followed some further discussion, during which Hook affirmed that he could in no way trespass on the kindness of a stranger, that he must leave immediately, and so on, while the host kept insisting that he join them. And so Hook sat down to a very fine meal and continued to entertain the guests with his wit for the rest of the evening.

An amusing prank. A little dishonest, perhaps, but mostly harmless — in return for his freeloaded meal, Hook gave his hosts an evening of entertainment.

Some of his other pranks were not so benign.

Hook's most famous — and most elaborate — joke, the "Berners Street Hoax" of 1809, is still remembered, more than two hundred years later. For some reason that history does not record, a Mrs. Tottenham, living at 54 Berners Street, in London, had earned Hook's displeasure. He, along with two accomplices, spent six weeks writing and mailing four thousand letters, ordering a wide range of food and merchandise, and inviting a large number of people, all to arrive on the same given date at Mrs. Tottenham's home.

The day began with several sooty boys showing up at the door, each having received a request for a chimney sweep. While the servant who answered the door was chasing them away, a number of large wagons heavily loaded with coal deliveries arrived, blocking the street. As the wagon drivers tried to sort out the mess, several cooks appeared, each carrying a large wedding cake. They were followed by waves of "tailors, boot-makers, upholders [undertakers] with coffins," and wagons delivering beer barrels.

As the coal wagons tried to extricate themselves from the congestion, a dozen carriages arrived, each expecting to take a married couple to their honeymoon. Then came doctors with instruments for amputation, lawyers, clergymen, and portrait painters. As each group arrived, they found the street to be thoroughly jammed, but nevertheless tried to force their way through to the front door to make their delivery and collect payment — none of the orders had been paid in advance.

By this time, it was noon. Forty fishmongers arrived, each bearing a large delivery of fresh fish, and then forty butchers with as many legs of mutton. At the peak of the chaos, as "the poor old lady grew to be bordering on temporary insanity," the lord mayor of London arrived. He was followed in turn by the governor of the Bank of England, the chairman of the East India Company, and the Duke of Gloucester.

How did Hook get *them* to show up?

Hook was well-connected and had access to all sorts of gossip. He knew enough stories about each of these four powerful visitors that he had been able to include in his invitation to each of them tempting insinuations that would force them to come. In his letter to the Duke of Gloucester, for example, he wrote that an old woman, formerly a lady-in-waiting to the King's mother, lay dying and had some confidential information (i.e., gossip) that she wanted to share with him.

Police were ordered to Berners Street in large numbers, to restore order. As they arrived, they ran into six large men delivering an organ, several barbers carrying new wigs, and a small army of dentists. Around five o'clock in the afternoon, while the police were still trying to calm everything down, a horde of out-of-work servants descended on the street from every direction, to apply for positions that had been posted. It was late in the evening when the street was finally brought back to normal.

Hook and his accomplices, who had rented the apartment across the street for the day and were watching the whole thing, must have found it all hysterically funny. But this was no harmless joke. There was the day-long disruption of the household and indeed the entire street, the large number of police who had to be occupied with trying to restore order, the stress on Mrs. Tottenham and her family and servants — and the very large number of butchers, bakers, coffin makers, fishmongers, and so on, all of whom lost money and time preparing and delivering goods they were never paid for.

Hook was strongly suspected of being behind the hoax, since he was so well known as a practical joker. Many tried to sue him for their losses, but there wasn't sufficient evidence and all charges were dropped.

His joking around was not just harmful to his victims. It eventually ruined his own life, too. He had many talents, including intelligence, quick wit, and charm. But he wasted these in a life of frivolity. He did get one civil service appointment, as government treasurer for the island of Mauritius, but he didn't take it seriously enough. It ended badly when one of his subordinates disappeared with cash worth over a million dollars in today's money, and Hook was held liable. He died at a fairly young age, severely in debt, leaving his wife and children more or less destitute.

There is a superhabit for dealing with the desire to have fun. The habit is called *Eutrapelia*, the habit of playing well — of having good leisure. *Eutrapelia* is a Greek word that means wittiness or liveliness. We use it because there's no English word that quite describes the habit of playing well.

The vice of "frivolity" opposes Eutrapelia from one extreme: *too much* playfulness. Frivolity tends to come in one of three types. The first is joking that is harmful or offensive. Hook's Berners Street Hoax is an example of this. The second type is joking around at the wrong time or place. Putting a fake spider on a friend's shoulder might be funny in a locker room, for example, but not in a courtroom. The third type of excessive playfulness is using your leisure time in ways that would undo any of the superhabits that you have developed. If you've spent weeks or months developing the superhabit of Restraint, for example, it would be contrary to Eutrapelia to spend your vacation giving in to every single desire, because you'd be undoing all your efforts to build Restraint.

The opposite extreme is having too little playfulness, or none at all. It is the vice of *mirthlessness*, the inability or unwillingness to relax, to enjoy leisure time. Mirthlessness *is* a vice, because playfulness is good for you. Studies show that playful adults have greater life satisfaction, for example. Too little playfulness can also cause serious problems.

As a young man, I was very ambitious. In college, I chaired the student union, led the debating team, and was the editor-in-chief of the college newspaper. After graduation, I became the youngest brand manager worldwide at Procter & Gamble. I then attended one of the highest ranked MBA programs in the world and graduated first in my class. After that I spent several years with the consulting firm of McKinsey and Company, working long hours and traveling extensively on assignments in the United States, Canada, Central and South America, Europe, and Russia.

Looking back, I think that a lot of that work was my way of avoiding thinking about significant areas of my life. My work got all my attention, and I had very little energy left over for the social, romantic, health, and spiritual dimensions of my life. In particular, I told myself that I had no interest in getting married and having children. Too much trouble, I thought. One colleague whom I respected said of his family, "I love them, but I have to admit that they're a burden." I concluded that I shouldn't get married; it didn't occur to me that the burden he described could be worth it.

John Garvey, former president of my university (and my former boss), in his book on virtue, gives a couple of good analogies for the kind of colorless, narrow, and plastic life I was living, with many of the best parts of reality missing. It was like Dorothy in Kansas before the tornado, in the *Wizard of Oz*; or like Harry Potter living with the

Dursley family, before he discovered that he was a wizard. Or, if you've seen the movie *Barbie*, it was like living in Barbieland. I had constrained my life down to work, and was living, as Thoreau said most people do, a life of "quiet desperation."

On a flight from New York City to my then hometown of Toronto, the cloud formation outside my window was a picture-perfect *cumulus fractus* — multiple broken clouds, at different levels. I could see all the way to the ground, through the sharply defined layers of clouds. I had a very clear perception of just how high we were. Suddenly, I had a vision of myself falling past those clouds, to my death.

What surprised me were my feelings as I experienced this vision: not of terror or panic, but indifference. Could I really have reached a point where I did not care whether I lived or died, when I was achieving all that I had set out to do? This cannot be good, I thought.

I realized that I needed to find something fun to do, that I needed to enjoy my life more. I spent some days thinking about this. I decided that I would really enjoy sailing. As a child, I had learned to sail from my older cousin Victor, and had happy memories of crewing for him. In quick succession, I took sailing lessons, rented sailboats, then bought my own boat and joined the Queen City Yacht Club on Toronto Island.

I started spending quite a bit of time on that boat, and got to know several people at the club. One evening, as I watched the city glow in the rays of the setting sun across Toronto Harbor with one of my new friends, I thought out aloud,

"You know, unlucky people spend their lives chasing after their goals, and never achieve them. But the *really* unlucky ones achieve their goals at an early age, and then have to face the emptiness that remains."

He agreed.

The following summer I took several weeks of unpaid leave from McKinsey, and lived on the boat and sailed around Lake Ontario, alone. It was a quiet, peaceful, contemplative, and very pleasant time. During that time, I started to consider all the other aspects of my life that I had been ignoring. I realized how much of life I had been missing.

A few months later, I resigned from McKinsey, sailed across the lake and then traveled via the Erie Canal, the Hudson River, and the Jersey Shore, to the Chesapeake Bay, and ended up in Annapolis, Maryland, and moved to Washington, D.C., to enroll in some further graduate study. There I met Kathleen.

We were married within a year, and today, as I write this, we are celebrating our twenty-seventh wedding anniversary. We have had six wonderful children together, and recently welcomed our first grandchild, Owen (whom you met in the Introduction).

The leisure time I had taken in the couple of years before meeting her allowed me to open my mind to this other, vitally important, dimension of life. The part of life that I had been deliberately excluding by working so hard has now become — by far — the richest part of my life. I had stumbled upon the power of Eutrapelia.

It's not just a question of giving yourself time to think about the larger questions of life — though spending quiet hours sailing, or hiking, or sketching does allow room for the big questions to pop up, so it's harder to ignore them. But there's something else going on, and it has everything to do with how our minds rest.

To rest from physical exhaustion, all you have to do is stop moving: sit down, or lie down. But that doesn't work for mental exhaustion. You can't just stop your mind. Even while you sleep, your brain continues to be active, particularly during rapid eye movement (REM) sleep.

So how do you let your mind rest? According to ancient and medieval philosophers, your mind rests during pleasant activities,

activities that you do for their own sake, the sorts of things we do during leisure time. Your mind is almost always working to achieve something. But when you're involved in doing something just for its own sake — just for the fun of it — then there's nothing for it to achieve. If your mind isn't trying to achieve anything, it can, in a certain sense, rest.

There is empirical evidence that leisure activities are good for your brain. For example, studies show that playing games can improve cognitive function, and that having hobbies can lower dementia risk. More generally, extensive research over several decades shows that leisure activities improve both mental and physical health. I think that Aquinas was spot on when he wrote that "enjoyment is rest for the soul."

Not having enough leisure prevents us from dealing with the bigger questions in our lives. It's not just that we don't have the *time* to deal with these questions. It's also that we don't have sufficient *mental energy* to engage with them. Leisure replenishes that energy.

What sorts of leisure activities are restful to your mind? And how do you determine what's the right amount of playfulness? First, avoid the three types of excessive playfulness discussed above: playfulness that is offensive, at the wrong time or place, or that undoes your efforts toward some other superhabit. If you avoid those, then all you have to do is choose something — anything — that you enjoy doing just for its own sake, where you're not trying to achieve anything. The sort of thing where, if someone asks you why you're doing it, your answer is simply, "Because I enjoy it."

Be careful, though. It is possible to have multiple motives for doing something. For example, you might work out at the gym because you enjoy it, but also for its health benefits. You could eat a meal for nourishment *and* for companionship *and* for the pleasure of it. Indeed, there may be many things that you do for some functional reason that you also enjoy. Ideally, we all enjoy significant parts of our work, our studies, and our chores.

However, unless your *primary* reason for doing something is that you enjoy it, then what you're doing doesn't count as leisure, in the sense that we're talking about here — in the sense of giving you mental rest. Your mind is at rest when it's not trying to achieve something, so if you're doing something primarily to achieve some result, not just for the joy of it, then it's not leisure. If you're trying to achieve something, then your mind is at work.

Even if you're trying to do something as simple, and apparently as mindless, as digging a hole in the ground, your mind is still working. Since you have a goal — a hole in the ground, of a certain size — your mind will be constantly checking to see how close you are to achieving your goal. *A little deeper ... a little more dirt out of this side ...* until you've achieved your goal.

And if you're thinking "I'm trying to achieve leisure," or "I'm trying to achieve mental rest," then you're missing the point entirely. Leisure, or rest for the mind, is exactly that thing that *cannot* be achieved. It only occurs when you are doing something you enjoy, just because you enjoy it.

Here's a way to figure out whether what you're doing is true leisure. Do you remember the Staples advertising campaign where people pushed a large red button labelled "Easy" and then the thing that they wanted done got done? If you had an Easy Button of your own, and pressing it would achieve the normal result of the activity you're doing, would you press it? If so, then it's not a leisure activity, at least not in the sense that we're talking about here: it's not giving you mental rest.

For example, would working out at the gym count as leisure for you? It depends. Try the Easy Button test: if you could push a button and get the health, strength, and physique benefits without going to the gym, would you push that button and stop going to the gym? If your answer is yes, then going to the gym isn't really leisure time for you. It's just another kind of work. That's not a bad thing. It might be fun work. But it's not leisure. Your mind is not resting because you're trying to achieve something.

Here's another issue: some potential leisure activities do require work *before* they can serve as leisure for you. When you first try to learn how to play guitar, for example, it's going to take work. But at a certain point, you become good enough that you can just pick up the guitar and start playing, and the main reason you do it is for the fun of it. Yes, each time you play it, you're practicing, so you're getting better. But that's no longer the main reason that you're playing guitar. If the main reason you play guitar is now for the joy of it, then it's leisure, even if you are getting better each time you play.

The possibility of mixed motives means that there's a good chance that you could be deceiving yourself. You could be filling your life with enjoyable activities, which nevertheless each have their own goal. You socialize for networking purposes; you exercise to keep fit; you read to improve your mind; you listen to music because it pumps you up and gets you motivated to tackle challenges. All of these are good things, but none of them are leisure.

You need to find some activity that you'll enjoy just for itself, or you are running a serious risk of not having the mental energy to engage the bigger questions in life.

Here's another example. If you have a family, one of the best kinds of leisure is to have dinner together as often as you can, ideally several evenings each week. Research by the National Center on Addiction and Substance Abuse at Columbia University shows that family dinners make important contributions to parent-child relationships, including preventing drug abuse among teens.

My own experience, after twenty-seven years of marriage, is that the highlight of my day is usually our family dinner, even now after some of our older children have moved out. And when the older ones return for a visit, every dinner is a family reunion. Though the family dinner does have its functional benefits — we need nourishment (and it keeps our kids off drugs, apparently) — if I could push that Easy Button to provide the same nutrition, I absolutely would *not* push that button, because I get so much enjoyment from our family dinners.

So we have superhabits for play, as well as for literally everything in life. Why? Because there's no part of your life that doesn't deserve to be the best that it can be. The wisdom that we are rediscovering includes an integrated set of habits that cover *every* aspect of human life.

How can we know that there's a superhabit for every situation in life? Because of the genius of the medieval philosopher-monk Thomas Aquinas, and something to do with the child's game of "Twenty Questions."

#9

The Superhabits System

YEARS AGO, I WAS driving with a friend through a city that was new to both of us. She was navigating.

"Oh dear," she said at one point, "we're coming to a part on the map that's unknown."

"What do you mean, 'unknown'?" I asked, baffled.

"There's a question mark right here," she said, pointing down at the map. "It must mean that they don't know what's here on this part of the map." That made no sense to me. This was a major city, not some unexplored wilderness — if the mapmakers didn't know what was there, surely someone could have gone and found out?

Taking my eye off the road for a second, I glanced at the map. There was a question mark — and it meant "Tourist Information."

Can we identify all the superhabits you need to live our best life, or are we doomed to keep running into unknowns, into question marks on any map of the superhabits? Scientists have mapped the human genome and expect a whole host of benefits to arise from that effort — can we do the same?

For thousands of years, philosophers have written about what I'm calling *superhabits*. More recently, social scientists are doing so as well. Unfortunately, they can't seem to agree on how many there are. Epictetus had four; William Bennett includes ten, Benjamin Franklin, thirteen; Romano Guardini, seventeen; positive psychology has six or twenty-four, depending on how you define them, and my former boss John Garvey's excellent book has twenty-nine. Is there any way to find a complete list, without any "unknowns"?

I found the answer to this question in the work of Thomas Aquinas, the thirteenth-century philosopher-monk. The way Aquinas solved this problem was by offering a *system* of virtues, not just a list.

99

What's the difference? Here's an illustration of what I mean. In the previous chapter on Eutrapelia, I wrote about the boat I sailed to Washington D.C., where I met Kathleen. We sold that boat when our first child was born. In the intervening years we owned other, smaller, boats, but it was not until last year that we acquired a larger sailboat, with an inboard engine. Because this new-to-us boat was so old, I quickly had to get up to speed on marine diesel engine maintenance. I found a list of replacement parts online. I also found a schematic diagram of the engine, showing how all the parts fit together.

That diagram was so much more valuable to me than just the list of parts, because it showed the *system*, how it worked, and how all the engine parts connect to each other. If the parts list happened to be missing a part, I would never have known it. But if the schematic diagram was missing a part, that would become evident as I looked at it closely — *Hey, how is the water supposed to flow from the water pump to the heat exchanger? There's no hose between them.* (Incidentally, that's not a purely hypothetical example: after replacing the water pump some weeks ago, I forgot to re-attach that hose and a geyser of water burst over top of our engine.) Having a system, not simply a list, gives you assurance that the list is complete, and it shows you how everything fits together.

I believe Aquinas understood this. He presented the superhabits — the virtues — systematically in a way that demonstrates completeness, and that illustrates how the superhabits all work together.

To explain his approach, let me introduce you to a concept I learned as a young management consultant at McKinsey and Company. The main task of a management consultant is to solve problems for a client. To do this, the client's problem needs to be properly understood, which requires taking it apart and looking at the pieces.

"Your analysis isn't MECE" is one of the most crushing criticisms you can receive as a junior consultant at McKinsey. It means that you haven't adequately separated the business problem you're working on into its component parts. In order to do that, a business problem had to be carefully divided and sub-divided to make sure that every part of the problem was covered, and only once. There had to be no overlaps among the parts, and no gaps between them: they had to be Mutually Exclusive and Collectively Exhaustive, or "MECE."

To take a very simple example, let's say that you were trying to figure out why your client company was losing money. You might start by separating revenues and costs. Then you could sub-divide costs into fixed costs and variable costs, and so on. You would have to decide whether to include discounts as a deduction from revenues, or an addition to costs. You could do either, but not both, because then you'd have an overlap — you'd be counting the same thing in two places and so your analysis wouldn't be mutually exclusive. On the other hand, if you left out discounts entirely, then you'd have a gap in your analysis and it wouldn't be collectively exhaustive.

Reading Aquinas's "Treatise on the Virtues" carefully, I was amazed to find that he had developed a "MECE" analysis of all of human life. By disaggregating every aspect of life, he showed how there is a superhabit for each.

Aquinas's approach was much like the children's game "Twenty Questions." Did you ever play it? One person thinks of something and the other person gets to ask a maximum of twenty questions to figure out what it is. Each question has to be a yes or no question. Bigger than a bread box? Smaller than a house?

The secret to winning is to ask each question in a way that the answer divides up the remaining universe of possibilities into roughly two equal parts, thereby eliminating half of them. For example, the question "Is it alive?" will divide the universe into two parts, and the yes or no answer will exclude one of those parts. The question "Is it bigger than a bread box?" divides the universe by size into those things that are bigger than a breadbox and those that are smaller or the same size, and the answer will exclude one part.

If each time you ask a question that divides the remaining set of possible answers into two, and eliminates half, then in just twenty questions you can find one thing from among more than a *million* possible things. (Mathematically, 2^{20} is just over a million — 1,048,576 to be exact. If you take 1,048,576 and divide by two, repeatedly, twenty times, the end result will be the number one. Grab a calculator and try it.)

In a way, Aquinas played a game like twenty questions with life itself. He considered a human life, and kept dividing its aspects into two (and occasionally three or more) parts. By doing so, he showed how there is a superhabit for each.

For example, he first distinguished between the material and spiritual aspects of life (he was a monk, and so the spiritual side of life was very important to him). He then divided our material lives into our practical and our intellectual lives. The latter is when we think just for the sake of thinking and knowing things; the former is for everything else. He then divided our practical lives into thoughts, actions, and feelings. (Look how "MECE" this is: In your day to day living, is there anything that occupies your time, other than your thoughts, your actions, or your feelings? No. There are no gaps and no overlaps here.)

Brené Brown, based on her extensive research, describes eighty-seven different emotions in her book *Atlas of the Heart*. These include stress, anxiety, worry, excitement, admiration, reverence, envy, shame, perfectionism, and guilt. Her descriptions of each are helpful for trying to understand and sort out complex and shifting feelings.

Aquinas did something much simpler. He divided feelings into just two groups, those that attract us to things, or people — our desires — and those that push us away, or repel us — our fears.

Next he did something very insightful. He noticed that our everyday thoughts, actions, and these two kinds of feelings lined up with what the ancient philosophers called the cardinal virtues: Prudence (or Practical Wisdom), Justice, Fortitude (or Courage), and Temperance (or Self-Discipline):

✣ Practical Wisdom is the superhabit of making wise decisions. In our everyday lives, our thinking is mostly oriented toward making decisions; so Practical Wisdom is the superhabit for managing our thinking.

✣ Justice is the superhabit of being fair to others and treating them in accord with their dignity. Since most of our day-to-day actions are *inter*actions with others, Justice is the superhabit for managing our actions.

✣ Courage is the superhabit for moving ahead with what we need to do, even if we are afraid; so it is the superhabit for dealing with fear.

✣ Self-Discipline is the superhabit of only following our desires when it makes sense to do so; it is the superhabit for managing our desires.

Practical Wisdom, Justice, Courage, and Self-Discipline are really big superhabits. Together they encompass every part of your everyday life: your thoughts, your actions, and your feelings.

At the same time, they're so big and so wide-ranging, they can be difficult habits to acquire — which is where Aquinas's second great insight comes in. He noticed that each of these cardinal superhabits had several other superhabits associated with it, which collectively contribute to it. *Cardinal* comes from the Latin word *cardo*, which means hinge, or pivot. These four are pivotal because so many other superhabits turn on them. For example, the superhabits we have covered so far — Restraint, Humility, Diligence, Gentlefirmness, Forgiveness, Orderliness, and Eutrapelia — are all types of the larger superhabit of Self-Discipline. Collectively these superhabits (and a few others) build up to the superhabit of Self-Discipline. So the best way to grow in Self-Discipline is to focus on growing in one of the smaller superhabits, like Restraint, for example, or Forgiveness. Then move on to another, then another. Eventually, you will have acquired the superhabit of Self-Discipline.

In the next chapter, we'll see how all the Self-Discipline superhabits fit together. And in the following three chapters, we'll do the same for the superhabits of Courage, Practical Wisdom, and Justice, respectively. If you haven't done so already, take a look at the Anatomy of Virtue diagram that comes with this book to see a visual representation of how all the superhabits fit together. The clockwise sequence on the diagram starting from twelve o'clock is the order in which the various superhabits are presented in the book. This sequence is not arbitrary. Self-Discipline comes first, because without it you can't even begin to get anything meaningful done; you'll be captive to all your whims and desires pulling you in every direction. Courage comes next, because once you've started in a particular direction, if you don't have Courage every obstacle will just knock you down. Then Practical Wisdom, which is required to make good decisions. And finally, Justice is necessary so that all your interactions with others are good ones.

I don't mean to suggest that until you've mastered Self-Discipline, you shouldn't try to grow in Courage. It's just that if you have no Self-Discipline at all, you might want to think about starting there. But once you have some measure of the superhabit of Self-Discipline, you can work on Courage next.

The first seven superhabits that comprise Self-Discipline, from Restraint to Eutrapelia, are themselves organized in an order that makes sense. For example, growing in Restraint is a really good place to start growing in virtue because, as we saw in chapter 1, there are so many simple ways to cultivate it. When you've developed some significant degree of Restraint, then you can start to work on Humility. Humility will give you a clear-eyed view of the areas in which you need to grow.

In a sense, these first seven are an "on ramp" to the superhabit life. Choose the first superhabit in this sequence that you think you need to grow in. Use the tips presented in each chapter to start making the small changes that will have a big impact on your life. (You'll notice too that making progress in one superhabit will help with others too, because they're all interrelated). Once you've made good progress in your first superhabit, try working on the next one that you need to develop, in the order they're presented on the diagram and in this book.

Whatever challenge you're facing in life, there's a superhabit for that. And if you have struggled with growing in Self-Discipline in the past, here's why it is so difficult: as you'll see in the next chapter, there are fifteen different types of Self-Discipline, one for each of fifteen types of desire (desires to do things, to know things, to control things, etc.). Don't try to grow in all of them at once. Instead identify which of the fifteen desires you struggle with most, and therefore which superhabit would most benefit you right now — which would bring the most improvement to your life — and focus on cultivating that one first.

We've already seen the Self-Discipline superhabits for managing our desires to do, to know, to be in control, to work, and to play. We have other desires too, for food, drink, sex, for possessions, even for how we move and dress. Is there really a superhabit for each of these, too?

#10

Self-Discipline

SUNRISE, 6:48 A.M., ON Saturday, March 7, 2020. With the rest of the world locked down in response to the COVID pandemic, ninety-five competitors stand beside their boats on a sandy beach on the north shore of Tampa Bay. They await the 7:00 a.m. starting gun for the Everglades Challenge, a three-hundred-mile race down the West Coast of Florida, through the Everglades, to Key Largo. They will travel on a mix of kayaks and small sailboats. There are just two rules for this race: (1) no engines, and (2) each boat must be small and light enough to be carried or pushed into the water from the beach, above the high-tide line, by its crew alone.

The competitors are known as the Watertribe, and each individual has a tribal name. "Iron Bob" and his son "TheJuice," for example, are notorious for their speed and endurance. Iron Bob celebrated a recent birthday with a thirty-mile bike ride, followed by a nineteen-mile paddle, a seven-mile hike, and another eleven miles of paddling. "Sandybottom" is a veteran of some ten Everglades Challenges. She has since won the Ultimate Florida Challenge, a 1,200 mile circumnavigation of the state that includes a forty-*mile* portage to bridge the gap between the Atlantic and Gulf coasts.

7:00 a.m. passes, but the starting gun does not fire. The wind is blowing at near gale-force against the incoming tide, causing enormous rolling waves. The race organizer postpones the start to relocate it to the south side of the bay. The contestants have to pack up their boats and gear, and either cartop or trailer across the Skyway Bridge, but by mid-afternoon, they are all underway.

They have eight days to complete the course. They will battle the ongoing strong winds, contrary tides, sleep deprivation, and the wilderness of the Everglades — avoiding its pythons, alligators, and the occasional Nile crocodile (which are an invasive species in South Florida and can grow to be sixteen feet long).

Of the ninety-five contestants, more than half will drop out along the way. One will not survive.

What leads people to undergo such hardship and endure such risks?

Watertribers will tell you it's a number of things. The extraordinary people you meet. The mutual respect, encouragement, and camaraderie that arise from participating in a shared challenge. The adventure and sense of purpose. The connection with nature and the feeling of being in touch with "the real world, where, for a few days, you exist completely in the moment, wave by wave."

One Watertriber told me it's his annual *misogi*, the ancient Shinto purification ritual of hiking to and then standing under a very cold waterfall; the word now stands for any very difficult challenge that you take on voluntarily. Others called it a "battle to overcome the physical and mental demons," noting that "a little suffering and hardship remind you of how great we have it in our daily lives."

The interesting question is: Where do they find the Self-Discipline to prepare for and undergo such a challenge? An Everglades Challenge requires months of planning and training. Participants practice falling out of and getting back into their craft, capsizing and righting it, and boating in the worst kinds of weather as well as in complete darkness. That takes serious Self-Discipline.

There's no money or fame to motivate you. Only the occasional sailing magazine covers the event, which is why you've probably never heard of it, and first prize is just a free entry to next year's race.

It's not just a Watertribe thing. Around the world people exercise tremendous Self-Discipline participating in activities as diverse as extreme sports, entrepreneurship, journalism, and stand-up comedy, which can't be explained merely in terms of the possible financial benefits or ego boost. Where do they find this Self-Discipline?

It is helpful to understand what Self-Discipline really is. Self-Discipline, or self-control, is the superhabit for managing your desires. It is not, at root, the ability to impose your will on your actions, against your feelings. Rather, as we saw in chapter 4 on Diligence, Self-Discipline is the fine art of coaxing your desires into more productive directions, by carefully nudging them in small and repeated ways.

This, I believe, is how the Watertribers find the Self-Discipline they need. You take one large thing that you really want, for whatever reason — camaraderie, sense of purpose, connection with nature — and then you coach and guide any smaller desires you have that might push you in a contrary direction, such as staying at home and watching YouTube videos, back toward that one bigger goal.

Of course, it's worth asking why we should be trying to change our desires. After all, some people think that happiness in life comes from fulfilling your desires, not changing them. There's an entire tradition in psychology, called "desire theory," that says that the path to happiness is exactly this: satisfying your desires. So why tamper with them? Well, for one thing our desires can sometimes lead us to do things that we know are really stupid things to do. Sometimes I desire to say something, do something, eat something, that I know I'll regret afterward.

A rival theory, "objective list theory," argues that happiness comes not from fulfilling desires but from achieving something on a list of worthy pursuits, such as "career accomplishments, friendship, freedom from disease and pain, material comforts, civic spirit, beauty, education, love, knowledge, and good conscience." Competing in an Everglades Challenge could belong on this list.

Even so, we do sense intuitively that, however worthy our aims are, our happiness does involve fulfilling our desires in some way, and that ignoring or repressing our desires can be quite unhealthy. As we saw above, in our discussions of Diligence and Gentlefirmness, our desires are energy and can be used productively, even heroically, and should neither be wasted on frivolous stuff, nor extinguished.

Aquinas offers an understanding of desire that integrates the best of both of these theories, even though he was writing hundreds of years before either theory was developed. He realized that our desires can be unruly, and need to be cultivated, channeled, to flow in the right direction. Think of desires as wild horses. The goal is not to kill or hamstring them, but to tame them so that they can run as fast as they did when they were wild, but with you at the reins, guiding them in the direction you choose. Recent research supports Aquinas's view, showing that taming our desires is not only possible, but also productive.

How do we grow in Self-Discipline by taming our desires? As we saw in the previous chapter, Self-Discipline is one of the cardinal superhabits. This means that it encompasses several smaller superhabits. Rather than cultivating Self-Discipline directly, you can focus on cultivating one of these subordinate superhabits.

A medical analogy can help explain this. My wife Kathleen at one point suffered from chronic lower back pain. She went through a string of healthcare providers who tried medications, massage, and cortisone shots. Nothing seemed to work until someone finally recommended Dr. Alec Wong, chiropractor to D.C. United, Washington's Major League Soccer team. He noticed that the problem was with her psoas muscle, which extends from your stomach around to your back. Once he treated that, her back pain disappeared. Her previous healthcare providers tried to treat her whole back. Dr. Wong isolated the problem to her psoas muscle.

Trying to grow in Self-Discipline is like trying to treat your entire back. Focusing instead on growing in one of Self-Discipline's subordinate superhabits, like Restraint, for example, is a more targeted, and likely more effective, approach.

How do you decide which of the superhabits related to Self-Discipline you should focus on first? Working through Aquinas's MECE description of human life is the way to do this. (Referring back to the Anatomy of Virtue diagram will be helpful as we go through this.)

His first distinction was between the spiritual and material life, and the second was between the intellectual and practical life. Practical life is then divided into thoughts, actions, and feelings — and feelings are divided into feelings against (fears) and feelings for (desires). The cardinal superhabit of Self-Discipline, and its subordinate superhabits, are for dealing with desires. (The superhabit of Courage, which we'll explore in the next chapter, is for handling fears).

Aquinas identified fifteen superhabits that are associated with Self-Discipline. These themselves are grouped into two kinds: for physical desires — food and drink, sex, and possessions — and for all other, non-physical, desires. Non-physical desires can be further grouped into desires for "what" and "how": what we want right now, and how we want to live.

There are five superhabits, which we have already seen, for managing our "non-physical desires" for what we want. They are grouped into desires to do things, to know things, and to control things.

The desires to do things are of two kinds, to do small, petty things and to do great things, which are addressed by the superhabits of Restraint and Humility, respectively. (If you find yourself frequently wasting time and energy following useless impulses or overly grandiose plans, then focusing on the relevant one of these two would be a good place for you to start growing in Self-Discipline.)

The desire to know things is managed by the superhabit of Diligence. This is the one for you if you have difficulty learning new things and find yourself wasting time on trivia.

The desire to control things is managed by Gentlefirmness and Forgiveness, which address "anger in the moment" and "anger after the fact" respectively.

There are also five superhabits for dealing with our non-physical desires for "how" we want to live, and specifically how we like to work, play, move, and dress. We've discussed the first two, Orderliness and Eutrapelia, which address the "work" of making sure that things are in the right order and place, and the "play" of having restful leisure.

There are three other superhabits for dealing with desires for how you want to live. They are two for how you move, covering the social and health dimensions of movement, and one for what you wear. This may seem a little strange. Do we really need superhabits about movement or clothing? Well, if you want to live your best life, there should be no part of that life that doesn't have a habit for dealing with it with excellence — even how we move and how we dress.

There are two superhabits for how we move, and one for how we dress. The two superhabits of movement are Gravitas, which is about the social impact of our movement on others, and Suppleness, which is about the impact of our movement on ourselves and particularly on our health.

Gravitas

Gravitas is the superhabit of being graceful in your interactions with others. It's not about the *substance* of your interactions with others, which is covered by Justice and its associated superhabits, it's about your actual movements themselves. Gravitas addresses your desire to move, or not, in any given moment. For example, Gravitas concerns desires that could lead you to fidget, to slouch, to pick your nose, or any from a number of possible actions. Gravitas ensures that your movements are guided by your social intelligence, so that others are more likely to respect you and cooperate with you.

If this seems trivial, consider that the very first of the twenty-four rules that Dr. Jordan Peterson has published to date is "Stand up straight with your shoulders back." Peterson explains how holding better posture actually reduces anxiety: "People, including yourself, will start to assume that you are competent and able (or at least they will not immediately conclude the reverse). Emboldened by the positive responses you are now receiving, you will begin to be less anxious." Further, research by Dr. Amy Cuddy on "power posing" (popularized by her TED talk, which is one of the most viewed TED talks of all time) showed that an open "power" posture leads to greater confidence and actual increases in testosterone.

If you feel that a big challenge in your life right now is that people aren't respecting you and your work, or taking you seriously enough, perhaps Gravitas is the superhabit you should be working on. One way to start would be to follow the advice of Bruce Lee, the famous martial artist and movie star. He used to say, "It is not daily increase but daily decrease, hack away the unessential." He meant that you should focus on eliminating unnecessary motion to increase the efficiency, simplicity, and fluidity of your movement. Paying close attention to how you stand and move will get you started on the superhabit of Gravitas.

SUPPLENESS

The other superhabit of movement is Suppleness. It is related to Gravitas, because it is also about posture and movement. But while Gravitas is about the impact of your movement on others, Suppleness is about the impact of your movement — or lack of it — on yourself, and particularly on your health.

Dr. James Levine, director of the Mayo Clinic–Arizona State University Obesity Solutions Initiative, has coined the phrase "Sitting is the new smoking." He argues that sitting for extended periods of the day is more dangerous than smoking, and kills more people than HIV. The superhabit of Suppleness helps you address this.

I mentioned earlier that I have been learning about the Pilates system of exercise. I have found it to be very useful in growing in Suppleness. Any form of exercise will help, though. Elite military and athlete coach Dr. Kelly Starrett's encyclopedic book *Becoming a Supple Leopard: The Ultimate Guide to Resolving Pain, Preventing Injury, and Optimizing Athletic Performance* is a great reference guide.

MODESTY

The superhabit of Modesty is the habit of dressing well. It does not mean dressing to make yourself look frumpy or boring. It just means not letting your clothing mask or distract from the marvel of who you are as a person. You may not like it, you may think it's wrong, but research shows that what you wear has a significant effect on what others think of you and how they interact with you. This superhabit of paying attention to how you dress is an often-overlooked contributor to the superhabit of Self-Discipline.

The final set of superhabits of Self-Discipline are those for dealing with our physical desires. There are five of these as well.

Our physical desires include desires for food and drink, sex, and possessions. These are typically our strongest desires, because of their role in survival: if we don't eat, we die; if we don't reproduce, the human race dies out; if we don't have possessions like a home to live in or some form of transportation, life can be very difficult.

The superhabits of Abstemiousness and Sobriety are the habits of eating and drinking reasonable amounts. "Reasonable" means exactly that: feasting at appropriate times, fasting at others, and the rest of the time, consuming enough so that you'll get the energy you need and the enjoyment you want from your meals and libations, without causing yourself social or health problems. While all superhabits lead to great health, these two are the ones that most directly make you healthier.

ABSTEMIOUSNESS

Research indicates that individuals with the superhabit of Abstemiousness exhibit less frequent overeating, snacking, and eating unhealthy foods and consequently tend to have a lower risk of becoming overweight, obese, and having chronic digestive diseases, and, not surprisingly, are less likely to develop clinical eating disorders.

Increasing awareness of the present moment through mindfulness seems to lead people to make healthier eating decisions. So, Abstemiousness can be enhanced by practices like making a daily food log, eating while sitting (instead of standing, or on the run), eating without distractions, and even taking more time to chew your food. The popular app Noom can be a useful aid to Abstemiousness and healthy eating.

As a first step in cultivating the habit of Abstemiousness, consider the Japanese practice of *Hara hachi bu*. As the Cleveland Clinic explains,

> *Hara hachi bu* is a Japanese term meaning "Eat until you're 80% full.... When you look at your plate, decide how much might make you feel full, and then estimate what 80% of that amount would look like. Perhaps it's two-thirds of the food on your plate. Aim

to feel satisfied and not hungry anymore, rather than full....

If you frequently find yourself mindlessly eating portions that are too big, start by just leaving one bite behind on your plate!... Then, once you have really got the hang of it, try leaving two bites."

That, of course, is the way to grow in any superhabit. Start with a small, manageable step, repeat it until it becomes part of you, and then take the next step.

SOBRIETY

Research on Sobriety indicates that it is associated with physical health benefits such as increased energy, weight management, and mental clarity, as well as psychological benefits including emotional well-being, improved mood, and stability. It is also associated with decreased tension, depression, and self-consciousness.

Interestingly, studies show that consuming alcohol in moderate amounts reduces stress, increases happiness, and increases overall emotional expression, and has also been found to improve cardiovascular health through the reduction of stress-related neurological activity. (At the risk of stating the obvious, consuming small amounts of alcohol over the span of a few days is linked to better health outcomes than consuming copious amounts during a short period.)

Excessive alcohol consumption can lead to adverse short-term effects including injuries, risky behavior, and alcohol poisoning. Extreme amounts of alcohol use can cause chronic illnesses, such as high blood pressure, heart disease, memory problems, and mental health problems. Drinking habits can be improved by tracking consumption, adjusting drinking patterns, setting goals, and relying on peer support.

Some people will consume alcohol because of peer pressure. Carly Fiorina, the former CEO of HP whom we met in chapter 3, on Diligence, developed a useful strategy for handling this early in her career. Her favorite drink is gin and tonic. When she didn't want any more alcohol, she would order a gin and tonic — with no gin. It looked to everyone else like an alcoholic drink, but it wasn't. I have found this strategy to be helpful myself on occasion.

CHASTENESS

Sine Cerere et Baccho friget Venus. Aquinas quotes this famous line from the Roman playwright Terence — "Without Ceres and Bacchus, Venus gets cold" — in writing about the superhabit of Chasteness. Ceres is the goddess of the harvest, Bacchus the god of wine, and Venus is the goddess of love. The implication is that without food or wine, sexual desire wanes. Modern science proves what the ancients knew: studies show that fasting reduces sexual desire. Interestingly, while fasting reduces testosterone, it does not appear to reduce muscle mass or strength, which is reassuring for men who want to fast as a way to moderate their sexual desire, but not become scrawny.

Superhabits reinforce each other. Here we can see that the super-habits of Abstemiousness and Sobriety help the superhabit of Chasteness. Chasteness is the superhabit of enjoying healthy sexual activity, within the proper context. Studies show that individuals engaging in healthy sexual behaviors had lower anxiety, depression, and distress compared to those who did not. Research also shows that healthy sexual behaviors are correlated with improved physical health, including immune system, blood pressure, and cardiovascular health.

Chasteness before marriage helps keep marriages together. Extensive and much replicated research indicates that the more sexual partners one has before getting married, the greater the chance of getting divorced. Recent research confirms that this effect cannot be attributed to factors such as religion, age, attitudes to sex, and a long list of other factors, and therefore that it's something about having sex before getting married that increases the chance of divorce.

If any of this feels troubling, you may want to read feminist Louise Perry's book *The Case against the Sexual Revolution*, for an evidence-based critique of current sexual practices. If you're already convinced of that critique, and would like help growing in Chasteness, a good book is Jason Evert's *If You Really Loved Me: 100 Questions on Dating, Relationships, and Sexual Purity*.

The remaining two superhabits for handling our physical desires are for dealing with our relationship with things. They are Thrift and Contentment, which relate to our desires for the quantity and quality of things we want.

THRIFT

Thrift is the superhabit for being satisfied with the *quantity* of things I have. Research shows that it is associated with being less impulsive when buying things and more conscious about a product's value.

The superhabit of Thrift, paradoxically perhaps, is commonly evident among successful entrepreneurs. Whether it is Sam Walton, founder of Wal-Mart, David Packard, co-founder of Hewlett-Packard (HP), Dave Green, founder of Hobby Lobby, S. Truett Cathy of Chick-Fil-A, Bob Luddy, founder of CaptivAire, or H. J. Heinz, founder of the company that popularized ketchup, they all had this superhabit. Tim Busch, along with his wife Steph, built a portfolio of luxury hotels, among other successful businesses; my business school is named after both of them. Tim amassed his first substantial savings from his paper route and then a lawn mowing business. He spent much of those savings on his college education, but the superhabit of Thrift stayed with him and was key to building up his later businesses.

It appears that it is not the strong desire for more stuff that helps people get rich, but their ability to moderate that desire through the superhabit of Thrift. In fact, people who place a high priority on financial success alone tend to have lower well-being and mental health, and more behavioral disorders. Interviews by Tom Corley, who spoke to over two hundred millionaires, seem to confirm the importance of Thrift: Corley found that millionaires tended to be surprisingly thrifty, avoiding "lifestyle creep" where expenses rise as fast as income.

A good place to begin to develop Thrift is by creating and living by a budget. The most useful thing I have found for this, by far, is an app called You Need a Budget (YNAB). As a business professor and a former management consultant, I thought I knew about budgets. I tried to run our household budget according to Generally Accepted Accounting Principles (GAAP). This was a mistake, because those principles are complex and are designed for consistency and transparency — which are not priorities for home budgeting. What I needed was something simple that would keep focusing me on making sure that our spending matched our resources and priorities. I floundered until I discovered YNAB. It's outstanding. (I have raved so much about them that YNAB published my story on their website.)

CONTENTMENT

Where Thrift is about the *quantity* of things you have, Contentment is about their *quality*. It is the superhabit for avoiding wanting a lifestyle that is too luxurious.

An extensive review of twenty-three empirical studies of people living simpler lifestyles concluded that they have stronger romantic relationships, better friendships, stronger social connections, and overall greater well-being and happiness. Other studies show lower stress and improved quality of life, and links to psychological well-being. Research also shows a link with physical health, because a simple lifestyle has been associated with lower risk-taking behavior such as drinking and drug use.

Jason DeSena Trennert, whom we met in chapter 3, talks about how he learned a lesson about a simpler lifestyle. On one of his earlier business trips, he brought all kinds of fancy gadgets with him. His much more experienced travel companion looked at the "overstuffed mess" Trennert was carrying, and said "half-amused, half-disgusted":

"Players ... travel ... light."

Players travel light. There's your answer. Be a player, and travel light through life. Don't get bogged down with excessive embellishment. For some guidance and inspiration on building the superhabit of Contentment, take a look at Marie Kondo's celebrated book *The Life-Changing Magic of Tidying Up: The Japanese Art of Decluttering and Organizing.* It is just as much about living a simple, contented life as it is about getting organized.

SELF-DISCIPLINE

The fifteen superhabits that we just reviewed collectively add up to the superhabit of Self-Discipline. If you have been trying to grow in Self-Discipline and finding it hard, you now know why: it *is* hard. To grow in Self-Discipline requires growing in Restraint, Humility, Diligence, Gentlefirmness, Forgiveness, Orderliness, Eutrapelia, Gravitas, Suppleness, Modesty, Abstemiousness, Sobriety, Chasteness, Thrift, *and* Contentment. Trying to grow in Self-Discipline directly is trying to do all of this all at once! Don't do that. If you focus on just one superhabit at a time, you will actually make more progress, instead of getting frustrated.

Managing our desires, one kind at a time, is the key to growth in Self-Discipline. For example, the men and women who participate in the Everglades Challenge exhibit many of the superhabits of Self-Discipline we have just discussed: Restraint, in limiting other activities to make space for their extensive preparation and practice; Humility, in knowing their strengths and weaknesses, and knowing when to forge ahead and when to remain safely on shore; Diligence, in their planning and researching currents and tides, possible camping sites, and alternate routes; and Suppleness — just watch Sandybottom paddling her kayak, and you'll see a vision of elegance and power in each stroke that is rarely matched.

Yet Self-Discipline alone is not enough to get you through the Everglades Challenge, or through life. Recall that in addition to the feelings that attract us to things, our desires, we also have feelings that repel us from things: our fears. Fortunately, there's a superhabit for that too. The superhabit of Courage does not eliminate fear — nothing can do that. What it does is it keeps us moving forward *despite* our fears, and shows us how to turn our fears into productive energy.

#11

Courage

"NEVER GIVE IN, NEVER, never give in."

Those words of Winston Churchill's are often quoted as the shortest graduation speech in history. In actual fact they were not — they were just the *title* of Churchill's speech to the graduating class of the Harrow School, in 1941, in the midst of the Second World War. Part of the actual speech went like this:

> "Never give in, never give in, never, never, never, never — in nothing, great or small, large or petty — never give in except to convictions of honor and good sense. Never yield to force; never yield to the apparently overwhelming might of the enemy."

Some months after delivering that speech, Churchill launched a convoy that would demonstrate the ability to "never, never, never, never … never give in" to an astounding degree.

It was August 1942. The Mediterranean island of Malta, then part of the British Empire, was the last unconquered Allied outpost in Europe, and on the verge of surrender. It is a tiny island, only seventeen miles by six. But it was at that time — as it had been throughout history — a place of great strategic value. It lay right along the Axis (German and Italian) supply lines between Italy and North Africa. Like an unsinkable aircraft carrier, the island was a launching platform for planes that constantly attacked enemy supply ships, destroying a large proportion of them and dramatically weakening the Axis armies in Africa.

The island was unsinkable, but it was not necessarily unconquerable. Because Malta is only sixty miles south of the island of

Sicily, the airfields of the German Luftwaffe and the Italian Regia Aeronautica were literally just minutes of flying time away from Malta — and so the island itself was bombed nearly without ceasing. In 1941 alone, the island suffered over *one thousand* air raids, several each day.

The biggest problem in defending Malta was ensuring the delivery of the food and fuel the island needed to keep going. These supplies had to travel by convoy across a thousand miles of enemy controlled sea, from Alexandria in the East or Gibraltar in the West. That's about a week of sailing, under constant threat of attack from enemy planes, ships, and submarines.

In early 1942, several convoys were attempted, and ship after ship was sunk or had to turn back. In one case, two supply ships made it through, but, heartbreakingly, were sunk in the harbor before they could be unloaded. By early August, it was calculated that Malta had enough food and fuel to last to the end of that month — at which point the island would be forced to surrender or starve to death. Churchill decided to hazard one last attempt to supply the island.

"Operation Pedestal," as it was named, left Gibraltar on the ninth of August for the seven-day run to Malta. That date was chosen to coincide with the dark of the moon, so that, at least during the night, the convoy might evade attack. There were fourteen supply ships, escorted by two battleships, three aircraft carriers, and about thirty destroyers and other lighter ships.

One of the fourteen supply ships in the convoy, the SS *Ohio*, was a large — but also very fast — American oil tanker. She was new, 515 feet long, and built in Chester, Pennsylvania, for the Texas Oil Company (now Texaco) just two years earlier. She carried ten thousand *tons* of oil, the bulk of the fuel supplies being delivered by the convoy — fuel that was essential for keeping Malta's planes flying. She had been retrofitted with several anti-aircraft guns before departure.

At the time she was the largest, fastest, and strongest oil tanker in the world, and the most important ship in the convoy.

The first two days of the convoy were deceptively quiet. On the third day, the eleventh of August, a German U-boat (submarine) approached the convoy undetected. It fired four torpedoes at one of the aircraft carriers, the *Eagle*. All four torpedoes scored direct hits, and the *Eagle* sunk in five minutes. Amazingly, most of her more-than-one-thousand-person crew were rescued. But 131 crew members died in the explosions, and the loss of the *Eagle* was a major disaster.

On the fourth day, August 12, the ships were attacked by twenty German Junkers 88s bombers and more than one hundred other aircraft. While they were being bombed, an Italian submarine slipped by the smaller boats surrounding the *Ohio* and torpedoed her amidships. The explosion set the ship ablaze. Her crew shut down the engines, fought the fire, and were able to extinguish it. But the *Ohio* was left with an enormous hole in her side, twenty-five feet in diameter, and her main steering mechanism destroyed. Fortunately, she had an emergency steering mechanism that her crew was able to activate. They restarted her engines and were just able to keep up with the rest of the convoy.

Next came a wave of sixty Junkers 87s — the famous Stuka dive-bombers that make the frightful shrieking sound you hear in World War II movies. All sixty of them focused directly on the *Ohio*. They knew that she carried the bulk of the fuel supplies for Malta.

By this time, the convoy's aircraft carriers had turned back. With the *Eagle* sunk, the other two were considered too valuable to risk. Their departure meant that the convoy at this point had no air cover, and everything depended on the ships' anti-aircraft guns.

These guns did their work. Several of the Stukas were shot down. Gunners from the *Ohio* itself shot down one Stuka, which crashed into the sea right behind it, bounced onto the stern of the boat, and destroyed one of the anti-aircraft guns. An officer called the captain on the ship's telephone to tell him what had happened. The captain's response:

"That's nothing — we've had one sitting on our bow this past half an hour" — another bomber had crash landed right on top of the ship, destroying part of the bridge.

Two clusters of bombs then fell on either side of the *Ohio*. When you watch movies of naval battles, you see big splashes of water whenever bombs miss their target. The bombs do not explode when they hit the bottom of the sea. They detonate as soon as they hit the surface of the water, and send a blast wave — and shrapnel — in every direction, so a near miss can be almost as damaging as a direct hit. In this case, with multiple explosions on either side of her, the immense *Ohio* was lifted up out of the water. She came crashing down, her engines destroyed, appeared to be sinking, and her crew abandoned ship.

But the *Ohio* did not sink.

What would you do at this point? The *Ohio*, carrying ten thousand tons of fuel oil and clearly the center of the enemy's attention, is a floating bomb. If her crew had been unsure of the extent of the danger, they would have been made aware of it a little earlier, when a smaller tanker in the convoy exploded. Most of its crew died in the explosion. A few managed to escape by jumping into the sea — but many of these were burnt alive as the blazing oil spread over the water.

What did the captain of the *Ohio* do? He asked for volunteers to reboard the *Ohio*, and he got them. Even some sailors whose own ships had already been sunk beneath them volunteered.

The *Ohio's* engines were wrecked, so they tried to get her towed by one of the destroyers. But she was too heavy, and they couldn't make any forward progress. As they were trying, *another* air attack came in. The gunners shot down one of the dive bombers, but too late: he had already released his bomb, and the *Ohio* received another direct hit. This broke her keel. The crew abandoned ship a second time, but waited through the night to see what would happen to her.

At dawn, they could see that she was still afloat. The volunteer crew reboarded, again. With *two* ships towing her, they were able to crawl forward at five knots. No sooner were they under way when another air attack inflicted two more direct hits, one at the bow and one at the stern. The stern explosion destroyed her auxiliary steering, which made it even harder to control the ship while she was being towed. But they persevered and were able to keep making progress. The day ended without further damage, and they continued onward through the cover of night.

At 10:45 the next morning, the first wave of dive bombers arrived. Three more waves followed. Then suddenly, a most welcome sight appeared: sixteen Spitfire fighters flying in formation from Malta. The *Ohio* was now within reach of the Allied fighter bases there. The enemy bombers no longer had the skies to themselves. It looked like the convoy was saved. The Spitfires shot down three bombers, and scattered the rest.

All except one. It flew past the fighters, came up on the *Ohio* from behind, and dropped a one-thousand-pound bomb right at her stern. Just missing the boat, it hit the water right behind her. The explosion ripped a huge hole in the stern of the boat. The *Ohio* was now broken beyond repair and clearly sinking, barely forty-five miles from Malta. The crew abandoned ship for the last time.

The tragedy of losing her when they had come so far could scarcely have been bearable.

Yet we should ask this question: How did they make it so far? Where did those crew members get the courage to carry on through the ongoing attacks, and *twice* re-board the *Ohio*?

Courage is the superhabit for dealing with fear. It is not the *absence* of fear. Fear will come, and there's nothing you can do to prevent that. Courage is the habit of accepting the feelings of fear, reframing them as a challenge, and then continuing to do what you need to do, despite the fear. It is the habit that we see in firefighters, police, members of the armed forces, mothers about to give birth — and the crew of the *Ohio*. It is not something you are born with. It is developed, like every other habit, through repeated practice.

In previous chapters we saw how desire is a source of energy. Fear can be a source of energy too. Emotion fuels motion. By reframing a fearful situation as a challenge, we can use fear as fuel for our actions and achievements.

The story of the volunteer crew members of the *Ohio*, who kept reboarding the *Ohio* to keep her moving, is a case study of Courage at its finest. These volunteer crew members were in the merchant marine, not the navy, which meant that they had not enlisted with any idea of being shot at or bombed. Indeed, for many, this convoy was their first time facing enemy attack. Where did they find that Courage? The life experiences of one of the crew members give us a clue.

Fred Larsen was junior third officer on the SS *Santa Elisa*, one of the fourteen supply ships in the Malta convoy. When he was three years and nine months old, in one week Fred lost his father, mother, grandmother, and one of his sisters, all succumbing to the influenza pandemic of 1918. For a year after that, he lived with his Norwegian grandmother in Brooklyn, with his two remaining siblings.

At age five, he was sent to live in Norway with an uncle and aunt, on a remote, cold, and rocky coast. His uncle John often took him to sea, and the two of them became inseparable — until John died of a heart attack when the boy was fourteen.

At seventeen, Fred went to sea by himself, signing on as a deck hand on a tanker sailing to California and China. Eventually he returned to Norway and enrolled in a maritime college, fell in love, and got married. Soon after, when his wife was pregnant with their first child, he went back to sea to earn money to support his new family, with the plan of bringing them to the United States after the baby was born.

This was in the spring of 1939. War broke out a few months later, and on the very day of the Larsens' first wedding anniversary, Germany invaded Norway.

Fred faced numerous bureaucratic obstacles in attempting to get papers for his wife and newborn son to emigrate to the United States. Desperate, he even sailed to England to volunteer with the Norwegian resistance, to try to re-enter the country to rescue his family. But they wouldn't take him because, even though he had lived much of his young life in Norway, he wasn't a native-born Norwegian and they were worried about spies.

Larsen returned to the United States, and in 1941, was assigned to the *Santa Elisa*, delivering cargo to and from South America. With the bombing of Pearl Harbor later that year, and America's entry into the war, he received a crushing letter from the State Department informing him that his chances of bringing his wife back from Norway were at this point negligible.

In late July 1942, the *Santa Elisa* was assigned to the Malta convoy. At this point, Larsen hadn't seen his wife in three years — and he had a three-year old son whom he had never met.

A few hours before the *Ohio* received her last, terminal hit, Larsen and the *Santa Elisa* were engaged in a nighttime gunfight with enemy E-boats (high speed motor torpedo boats). The *Santa Elisa* was hit and set aflame by a torpedo, and Fred joined the surviving crew members in following the order to abandon ship. They spent the remainder of the night in life rafts, and were rescued by one of the convoy's destroyers the next morning.

That destroyer, the USS *Penn*, made rendezvous with the *Ohio*, which was lying broken and sinking after the thousand-pound bomb explosion had blown in her stern.

A third and final attempt was made to save the foundering tanker, although she was clearly sinking. The *Penn* and one other destroyer were lashed to either side of her to keep her afloat. In these last and most dangerous moments in the saga of this sinking ship, the *Ohio*'s volunteer crew reboarded her one last time.

Larsen joined them, stepping across from the *Penn* to the *Ohio*. His own ship had sunk under him, and he was under no obligation to do this. No one asked him to do it. He just went aboard and manned one of the *Ohio*'s guns.

Courage, like Self-Discipline, is one of the four cardinal superhabits. The remaining two are Practical Wisdom and Justice, which we'll discuss in the next two chapters. We saw previously how each one of these cardinal superhabits has a host of subordinate superhabits: Self-Discipline has fifteen. Courage has four (as you'll note on the Anatomy of Virtue diagram).

Courage is all about dealing with challenges, and specifically, the fear that can arise when we face a challenge. There are two kinds of challenges in life, those that can be overcome, and those that can't, at least in the short term, and simply have to be endured. Accordingly, the superhabits related to Courage are divided into these two groups, with two superhabits for dealing with challenges that can be overcome, and two for those that must be endured.

The two superhabits for challenges that can be overcome are, very practically, related to those that can be solved by spending a lot of money, and those that require lots of human effort.

MUNIFICENCE

Munificence is the superhabit of being willing to spend large sums of your own money in order to achieve a great good, or to solve a great problem. It is different from Generosity. Generosity is also a superhabit, but it is related to the superhabit of Justice, which we'll discuss in chapter 13. Because Munificence involves large sums of money, it is the only superhabit that cannot be cultivated by everyone. You need to already be wealthy to cultivate it, because giving away someone else's money is not a virtue.

Munificence is appropriately associated with Courage: ironically, the more money you have, the more you usually fear its absence. Studies on loss aversion (where the pain of a financial loss weighs more than the pleasure of an equivalent financial gain) conclude that wealthier people are more loss averse. Giving away large portions of your wealth takes Courage. But like the rest of the superhabits, it comes with a host of benefits.

Research on individuals who donate money to others found that they experienced increases in psychological well-being and happiness. Other research on giving money and social support showed that they are associated with better overall physical and psychological health in adults. Still other research showed that individuals who donated or gifted money to others were more likely to be less stressed and happier in the future. Giving away large sums of money is good for you.

Interestingly, giving doesn't seem to suffer from diminishing marginal utility, where each additional unit gives you a smaller increase in pleasure (for example, eating a third donut doesn't give you the same joy as eating the first). Donating the same amount repeatedly *does* appear to provide the same psychological benefits each time.

Like every other superhabit, Munificence is developed through practice. I have two good friends, a lovely couple, who made a fortune of hundreds of millions of dollars. They have decided to give it all away to support K–12 education. They cultivated the superhabit of Munificence by starting to give away significant sums of money early, *before* they accumulated significant wealth.

MAGNANIMITY

What if you're not wealthy, or if the challenge you'd like to address cannot be solved just by spending money? Magnanimity is the superhabit for dealing with large challenges *without* spending lots of money. The word comes from the Latin phrase *magna anima*, which means "big soul." It's the habit of "big-souledness," the spirit of diving in and energetically taking on a big challenge.

Research on cancer patients suggests that increases in Magnanimity can reduce levels of psychological distress, including reduced depression and anxiety, and that Magnanimity can be increased by exposing oneself to inspiring case examples and stories.

Alexandre Havard's excellent book *Created for Greatness: The Power of Magnanimity* provides a helpful book-length treatment of this superhabit. He explains how Magnanimity is the leadership superhabit *par excellence*, because it allows us to take on great challenges.

The remaining two superhabits of Courage are for dealing with challenges that cannot be overcome, and simply have to be endured. They are for handling physical and mental challenges, respectively.

PERSEVERANCE

A chronic illness, in yourself or a loved one, is an example of a challenge that cannot be overcome, and must be endured. It takes a certain type of Courage to do that, and we call it Perseverance, the superhabit for enduring physical challenges.

Also known as grit, studies show that Perseverance is linked to a higher quality of life and to happiness. Individuals who possess a high degree of Perseverance have the ability to learn from failures and delay gratification. Individuals who practice Perseverance and have a positive outlook are at a lower risk for depression, anxiety, and panic disorders. Individuals who consistently have a positive outlook and persevere through obstacles tend to have a growth mindset, allowing them to continue pursuing their goals in the face of adversity.

Research indicates that Perseverance can be improved through pursuing something you care deeply about, since you're more likely to overcome setbacks if you have an interest in the goal.

Persevering in the face of physical challenges builds the superhabit of Perseverance. Giving up in the face of such challenges does the opposite: as former defense secretary Donald Rumsfeld used to say, "Once you quit one thing, then you can quit something else, and pretty soon you'll get good at being a quitter."

RESILIENCE

The second habit for enduring a challenge is Resilience, the superhabit for enduring mental challenges like sorrow, anxiety, and depression.

Resilience is yet another superpower. It is associated with improved health outcomes and serves as a predictor of mental and physical well-being in multiple domains of life. One study on Resilience and high-strain work environments found that workers with high Resilience have lower depression, stress, and burnout rates compared to those that have low Resilience. Another study found that increased Resilience was associated with psychological well-being in elementary-age children. In the brain, Resilience correlates with increased activation in the prefrontal cortex and lower activation of the amygdala, the area of the brain associated with fear and stress response.

Studies also show that Resilience can be increased, and interventions aimed at increasing Resilience have had positive effects on people's physical and mental health. A randomized-controlled trial of a Resilience training approach in adults with Type 2 diabetes found that those receiving the Resilience intervention developed positive ways of coping with diabetes-related stress, ate healthier, exercised more, and had a better outlook on life compared to the control group.

Surviving in succession the deaths of loved ones, the hardships of life at sea, and separation from his wife and child, Fred Larsen had had numerous occasions to practice both Perseverance and Resilience. Each time he found the energy in his fear or sadness to move on, he built up the superhabit of Resilience; each time he kept moving forward — despite tiredness, cold, or danger — he cultivated the superhabit of Perseverance. And each time, he made it easier to be resilient, persevering, and courageous the next time around. That is how he developed the strength to endure the sleepless nights, gunfire, and bomb blasts as the convoy crossed the western Mediterranean.

Fred's decision to board the *Ohio*, though, was an act of Magnanimity. Perseverance and Resilience helped him endure. But here was a chance to overcome — to help bring this prized tanker the last few miles to her destination. The order was "to bring the *Ohio* in at all costs," he said later. So that's what he did.

They were under almost constant attack. The air cover helped, but the enemy was now sending fighter planes to engage Malta's Spitfires so that the Axis bombers could get through. The *Ohio* continued to sink. At this point, her amidships deck was only three feet above the water. According to Larsen, "By now there was mostly dive-bombers comin' in, and they were comin' in very fast, especially in the morning and late in the afternoon.... You could hear them quite a distance away, so we knew they were comin.'"

Somehow, the volunteer crew was able to keep the *Ohio* going.

At 9:30 a.m. on the seventh day, the *Ohio* was dragged into the Grand Harbor at Malta, her deck now at sea level, the two destroyers barely holding her up. Half the island showed up to cheer her in. One hundred thousand people lined the walls of the city. The dock workers were able to pump out all the oil from the *Ohio*. As the last few gallons left her, she broke in two, and sank to the bottom of the harbor, her mission complete.

The success of the convoy meant that Malta was able to continue the fight. Bombers from the island stopped much of the supplies to Field Marshal Rommel in North Africa, leaving him critically short of fuel and contributing to his defeat at the battle of El Alamein — a key turning point in the Second World War.

Fred Larsen's wife Minda and their son eventually made it to the United States. When Fred returned, he was finally reunited with his family. He participated in a total of sixty-five convoys throughout the war, and for his actions in the Malta convoy, he received the Merchant Marine Distinguished Service Medal, the highest award the branch can give, "for heroism above and beyond the call of duty."

Minda and Fred had another child, a daughter, and they spent a happy life together in New Jersey, until Fred passed away peacefully in 1995, aged eighty. In what turned out to be the last year of his life, he was invited to give a talk about his experience to his local chapter of merchant marine veterans. It was the only time he ever spoke publicly about the Malta convoy.

As the subject of his remarks, he chose Courage, and the example of Courage he gave was Minda.

After Fred died, Minda lived for another twenty-six years, until 2021, to age 104. By then, she had five grandchildren, ten great-grandchildren, and two great great-grandchildren.

The story of the Malta convoy has great personal meaning for me. I grew up on the island. My father (who was a little boy at the time) and my grandfather were part of that crowd, cheering like crazy as the *Ohio* limped in. The freedom of the islanders — and perhaps their lives — was saved that day, by the courage of men like Fred Larsen.

It is an inspiring story. Yet developing the superhabits of Perseverance, Resilience, and Magnanimity does not require the crucible-like environment that was Fred Larsen's childhood. Daily life contains plenty of occasions where the superhabit of Courage is required, plenty of occasions that can generate fear. These moments are when fear can be reframed and used as energy to grow in Courage through its allied superhabits.

Reframing is a simple but powerful tool that recognizes that fear, and anxiety in particular, is "adrenaline with a negative frame." Adrenaline is a performance-enhancing hormone. Reframing replaces the negative frame with a positive one, and repurposes adrenaline in a more constructive direction. It's not just a mind game — reframing can have an immediate positive physiological impact. For more on this, listen to the *Optimal Work* podcast #193, "Mindset Mistakes That Sabotage Success."

The point is not to compare your level of courage to Fred's, or to anyone else's. The point is to use the everyday fears that invariably arise in life to grow in the superhabit of Courage. And remember, with superhabits, beginning is winning, because you'll experience the benefits as soon as you start practicing them.

When researchers track what happens to people as they grow in Resilience, for example, they see concurrent improvements in both mental and physical health. Dr. Mary Steinhart at the University of Texas at Austin has developed a program called "Transforming Lives through Resilience Education," which includes four modules, each with a video and a short interactive quiz. One study of college students who participated in this program showed that they developed more effective coping strategies, higher self-esteem, and lower symptoms of depression and stress after just three months, compared to a control group who did not participate in the program.

Here's a simple exercise that anyone can use to grow in the superhabit of Resilience, as described by Jia Jiang in his popular TED talk and his book *Rejection Proof*. Many people fear rejection, and this can get in the way of growing in Resilience. If you are one of them, this is Jia's rather amusing approach. Once a day, for thirty days, ask someone for something where you know that the answer will be no. Start simply — go to a clothing store and ask if they sell a brand that you know they don't sell. If you're a student, ask a professor for an extension on your assignment, if you know that she typically doesn't allow that. Try this kind of question for a few days.

When you get used to hearing the word *no* without wincing, then you can move on to harder questions. Examples that Jia tried: ask a stranger to borrow one hundred dollars. Ask for a "burger refill." Ask a donut shop if they could sell you five donuts linked just like the Olympic symbol. (This last one "backfired" for Jia when a keen Krispy Kreme employee actually did it.) After thirty days of this exercise, you will have begun to build Resilience — you'll be able to ask for things without as much fear of rejection as you used to have. And that's a very good place to begin growing in Resilience.

Courage, like every superhabit, is the mean between two extremes. It requires paying the right amount of attention to your fears. Too much attention to fear, and you fall into the vice of cowardliness. Too little attention, and you have the opposing vice of rashness. The wisdom to know the difference is what the next cardinal superhabit is about: knowing *when* to abandon ship, and when to reboard.

Or when to land the plane, and when to ditch it …

#12

Practical Wisdom

On a cold January afternoon in 2009, U.S. Airways Flight 1549 ran into a flock of geese shortly after takeoff that, in a rare case of extremely bad luck, wrecked both of its engines. Captain Chesley "Sully" Sullenberger became famous for landing that plane in an impossibly difficult situation. Less well known are the many moment-by-moment decisions that he made during the crisis, and how he had prepared for such an emergency. The 19,633 hours of flight time that he had under his belt at that point, 4,765 of which were on Airbus A320s, the type of plane he was flying that day, were part of that preparation. It was also his life-long development of the superhabit of Practical Wisdom that enabled him to respond so effectively in such an intense situation.

Since they were still at such a very low altitude, they had about *three minutes* before the plane would crash into downtown Manhattan, killing all 155 passengers and crew aboard — as well as potentially hundreds, perhaps thousands, more people in the crowded city below.

Practical Wisdom is the superhabit of making and implementing wise decisions, whether well-deliberated, strategic decisions over extended periods of time, or near-instantaneous ones like the ones Flight 1549 faced. Both *making* and *implementing* decisions are equally important parts of Practical Wisdom. This is not "theoretical wisdom." It is not making a decision and then filing it away. In a very real sense, Practical Wisdom recognizes that a decision is not properly made until it is implemented.

The plane had to be landed safely. And soon.

Practical Wisdom is sometimes referred to as *Prudence*, from the Latin word *prudentia*. However, like so many other virtue-related words, Prudence has come to mean other, very different things, including "cautious," "discrete," "timid," even "prissy." Practical Wisdom is not any of these things: it involves a firm grasp of reality; gathering the available, relevant information needed to make a decision; reasoning through this information; drawing practical conclusions; and then turning those conclusions into action, even — indeed, especially — amidst uncertain, changing conditions.

Like self-discipline and Courage, it has several component superhabits. According to Aquinas, there are eight of these: four for gathering the relevant information, one for reasoning, and three for implementing. (Aquinas was writing 750 years ago; but it is remarkable how closely his framework matches, and yet goes deeper than, many contemporary decision-making processes.)

If we review the progress of Flight 1549, moment by moment, in the light of these eight superhabits, you'll see how Sully had developed the virtue of Practical Wisdom to a high degree and how he applied it to this drastic situation.

3:24:54 P.M. — Cleared for takeoff

US Airways Flight 1549 departed New York's LaGuardia airport, with first officer Jeff Skiles flying, bound for Charlotte, North Carolina.

3:25:45 P.M. — 51 seconds after takeoff

The plane reached seven hundred feet of altitude. Skiles reported in to the control tower, and he was instructed to continue to climb to fifteen thousand feet. The skies were clear, and they had a beautiful view of the New York skyline and the Hudson River below.

3:27:10 — 2 minutes 16 seconds after takeoff

Sullenberger and Skiles both saw a large flock of birds. Almost immediately, the sounds of "thumps and thuds" could be heard in the cockpit — and, a second or two later, of engines slowing down rapidly. What should they do next?

There was very little time to decide. For perspective, unless you are an exceptionally fast reader, in the time you've taken to read this far in the chapter, Flight 1549 had taken off, hit the birds, and crashed into Manhattan. It all happened that quickly.

But let's "freeze" the plane in mid-air while we explore the situation in the light of each of the eight superhabits of Practical Wisdom.

The first four superhabits that make up Practical Wisdom are for assembling the information needed to get a firm grasp of reality. Two of these are for recalling existing information, and the other two are for acquiring new information.

The existing information can be of two kinds — data and principles.

MEMORY

Existing data are gathered through the superhabit of Memory. Is memory actually a habit? There is a complex scientific literature on what exactly memory is, which we don't need to dive into here. What is clear is that it certainly acts like a superhabit, in three significant ways: repeated practice can improve your memory; a good memory has a wide range of benefits; and improvements in memory lead to greater mental health and happiness.

The important thing about the superhabit of Memory is that it be *reliable*. Reliable information is required for sound decision-making; faulty information will lead to faulty decisions. Aquinas offers four suggestions for how to remember things reliably:

1. Organize what you want to remember into a logical structure that will make it easier to remember.

2. Be enthusiastic, even anxious, about what you want to remember; it will set it more firmly in your memory.

3. Make "some suitable yet somewhat unwonted illustration of it, since the unwonted strikes us more." (That is to say, by making a funny or unusual image in your mind of what you want to remember, you will make it more memorable.)

4. Reflect often on the things you want to remember, which will fix them in your memory.

Collectively, these four strategies allow you to create a strong mental model of what you are trying to remember.

Captain Sullenberger had decades of flying experience. He took lessons as a teenager, joined the Air Force and became a fighter pilot, and later became a commercial pilot. From early in his flying days, he also had a strong interest in flight safety, and had studied numerous aerial crises and how to deal with them.

His flight training gave him theoretical frameworks to organize his thoughts about his experience, and his lifelong enthusiasm for flying strengthened his recollection of what he needed to know.

Sully also had some jarring images seared in his memory. In one early case, while he was still taking his first flying lessons, he had the occasion to observe up close, on the runway that he used for his practice, the remains of a fatal plane crash that had occurred a couple of days earlier. The pilot had come in low, swerved upwards to avoid some previously unnoticed powerlines, stalled, and plummeted headfirst into the airstrip.

Sully recalled:

> [I] looked inside at the blood-spattered cockpit.... I
> tried to visualize how it all might have happened — his

effort to avoid the power lines, his loss of speed, the
awful impact. I forced myself to look inside the cockpit, to study it.... It was a pretty sobering moment for
a sixteen-year-old.

For the purposes of Practical Wisdom, reliable recall is most beneficial
if the experiences recalled are themselves of excellent quality. Memory
of thousands of hours of average quality flying experience will not be
as valuable as the memory of hours of focused effort on highly skilled
flying, cultivated to perfection. As coach Vince Lombardi was sup-
posedly fond of saying, it's not "practice makes perfect" but *perfect
practice makes perfect.*"

This is the kind of experience that Sully had, as one can see from
his account of another flight some years before Flight 1549.

I had piloted an Airbus A321 from Charlotte to San
Francisco. It was one of those nights when there
wasn't much traffic. Air traffic controllers didn't have
to impose many constraints about altitude or speed. It
was up to me how I wanted to travel the final 110
miles, and how I would get from thirty-eight thousand
feet down to the runway in San Francisco.

It was an incredibly clear and gorgeous night, the air
was smooth, and I could see the airport from sixty
miles out. I started my descent at just the right distance so that the engines would be near idle thrust
almost all the way in, until just prior to landing. If I
started down at the right place, I could avoid having to
use the speed brakes, which cause a rumbling in the

cabin when extended. To get it right, I'd need to per-
fectly manage the energy of the jet.

"It was a smooth, continuous descent," he later told his wife, "one
gentle, slowly curving arc, with a gradual deceleration of the airplane.
The wheels touched the runway softly enough that the spoilers didn't
deploy immediately because they didn't recognize that the wheels
were on the ground."

> I'm guessing that no-one on the plane even noticed.
> Maybe some people sensed it was a smooth ride, but
> I'm sure they didn't think about it. I was doing it for
> myself.

As a result of this ongoing striving for perfection, Sully had the experience he needed when the crisis came.

> I had spent years flying jet airplanes and had paid
> close attention to energy management. On thousands
> of flights, I had tried to fly the optimum flight path. I
> think that helped me more than anything on Flight
> 1549. I was going to try to use the energy of the Air-
> bus, without either engine, to get us safely to the
> ground ... or somewhere.

JUDGMENT

In addition to committing our experience to memory, we also draw
lessons from it; this refines Judgment, the superhabit of knowing
what principles should operate in the particular situation. The
operative principles in an air emergency, as Sully learned them in
the Air Force, are (1) maintain aircraft control, (2) analyze the

situation and take proper action; and (3) land as soon as conditions permit. The training also taught that in such circumstances the first officer should usually fly the airplane, to free the captain up to analyze the situation: "It is usually optimal for the first officer to fly so the captain can think about the situation, make decisions, and give direction."

Sully had studied cases like this. United Airlines Flight 811 from Honolulu to Auckland, New Zealand, which suffered a catastrophe in mid-air when the forward cargo door blew out, is one that stands out.

"A huge hole was left in the cabin, and two of the engines were in flames, severely damaged by debris ejected from the plane during the incident," he later recollected. The pilot shut down the burning engines, and had to figure out how to return safely to Honolulu on the remaining two engines. Procedure in this case required the pilot to pull the fire shutoff handles, but he did not do so. He realized that "if he did so, two hydraulic pumps would be lost, which would affect the crew's ability to maintain control of the aircraft. So he did not pull them." This gave him the control he needed to return the plane to a safe landing. Sully had learned that "Not every situation can be foreseen or anticipated. There isn't a checklist for everything."

Procedure said that the first officer should usually fly the airplane in an emergency. But Sully's judgment said that this was one of those unusual cases when the captain should take over:

> Even in those early seconds, I knew that this was an emergency that called for thinking beyond what's usually considered appropriate. As a rush of information came into my head, I had no doubts that it made the most sense for me to take the controls.

3:27:23 — 2 MINUTES 29 SECONDS SINCE TAKEOFF

"My aircraft," he said, and took over. He then asked the first officer to grab the Quick Reference Handbook (QRH) to look up the checklist for "loss of thrust on both engines." We don't always have all the information we need to make a good decision. When that's the case, there are two ways to acquire the information we need: to learn it from another source, or to discover it for yourself.

TEACHABILITY

Getting new information from another source requires an openness to learning, and this is the superhabit of Teachability. It is the habit of being able to learn well from others.

Teachability is related to, but distinct from, the superhabits of Diligence and Humility, both of which we saw earlier. As you'll recall from chapters 2 and 4, Humility is an accurate assessment of your own abilities, including what you know and don't know, and Diligence is a harnessing of the desire to know. Teachability, by contrast, is an openness to learning, arising from a commitment to grasping the reality of things. It takes Peterson's rule nine, "Assume that the person you are listening to might know something you don't," and turns it into a habit.

The QRH is an important resource. The complexity of a modern aircraft is such that you cannot commit the procedures for dealing with every kind of emergency to memory. Accessing it immediately to learn what to do is a necessary first step. Far more important to the safety of the passengers and crew was how teachable Sully had been throughout his entire life — a mid-air crisis is not the time to be learning many new things.

Sully learned to fly at age sixteen in North Texas, from a cropdusting pilot, L. T. Cook. While Cook didn't speak much, he seemed to like Sully's seriousness and quiet enthusiasm, how he listened carefully, watched closely, asked questions, and studied hard. After sixteen lessons, Cook recognized that the teenager had mastered the basics, so he sent him up for his first solo. It went smoothly, so he allowed Sully to rent the plane and practice alone whenever he liked for the rest of the summer. Sully did so, enthusiastically.

Years of training and flying experience followed, first in the Air Force and then as a civilian pilot.

One important way Sully demonstrated the superhabit of Teachability was his determination to learn from others' mistakes. He wrote, "I had closely studied other airline accidents. There is much to be learned from the experiences of pilots who were involved in the seminal accidents of recent decades. I have soberly paged through transcripts from cockpit voice recorders, with the last exchanges of pilots who didn't survive." This lifetime of learning from others was put to good use on Flight 1549.

> In many ways, all my mentors, heroes, and loved ones — those who taught me and encouraged me and saw the possibilities in me — were with me in the cockpit of Flight 1549. We had lost both engines. It was a dire situation, but there were lessons people had instilled in me that served me well. Mr. Cook's lessons were a part of what guided me on that five-minute flight.

3:27:33 PM — 2 MINUTES 39 SECONDS SINCE TAKEOFF

Sully issued a "Mayday" call to the control tower, and informed them that they were turning back to La Guardia. They went through the QRH checklist steps for loss of thrust, and attempted to restart the engines. But the engines would not reignite. Air Traffic Control cleared the runways at La Guardia Airport, and offered runway 13, which required the plane to make a sharp turn to get back to the airport.

3:28:49 — 3 MINUTES 55 SECONDS SINCE TAKEOFF

At this point it became clear that they wouldn't be able to reach La Guardia airport. Sully inquired about Teterboro airport, a smaller airport on the other side of the Hudson which served mainly private planes. A runway was cleared for them there. But they soon realized that that wouldn't work either:

"We were too low, too slow, too far away, and pointed in the wrong direction, away from nearby airports."

They needed another idea.

CREATIVITY

The second superhabit for acquiring new information is Creativity, gaining new information by discovery. Creativity, like every other superhabit, can be learned by anyone. If you think, "I'm just not a creative person," it's just because you haven't yet started to develop this superhabit. Anyone can do it.

A necessary first step is to let go of any false beliefs about Creativity, such as the wrong-headed idea that to be creative you must eliminate all boundaries. In fact, we know that the right kind of structure actually improves Creativity.

As a persuasive example of this, while we keep Flight 1549 frozen in mid-air, let's consider the case of another interrupted, though less dire, voyage. Joanne was stuck on an evening train home to London, badly delayed. As she stared out of the window, all of a sudden, several ideas for different characters in a magical world came to her. As she described it,

> It was the most physical rush of excitement. I've never
> felt that excited about anything to do with writing.
> I've never had an idea that gave me such a physical
> response. By the end of that train journey, I knew it
> was going to be a seven-book series.

This story of the birth of Joanne (J. K.) Rowling's Harry Potter series is legendary.

It is commonly believed that the entire series fell, as a flash of creative insight, more or less fully formed, into her head on that train ride. All she had to do is write it down. But that's not at all how it happened.

Rowling spent the next five years plotting out each of the seven books. She was very meticulous in thinking through each part of each book. She developed fifteen different variations of the first chapter of the first book alone. She laid out a chart that included every single character in Harry Potter's class at Hogwarts School of Witchcraft and Wizardry, which she used to develop her plots. As she planned each book, she listed the chapters, and subplots in each chapter, and a map to show how the various subplots would unfold.

This appears to be the case with most successful creative work: that it is much more about iteration and development than a single, blinding flash of inspiration. Indeed, even though we describe such inspiration as a "light bulb moment," the actual development of the lightbulb itself by Thomas Edison did not come in a moment of insight — it was the result of over a thousand iterations.

In the case of Flight 1549, because all the known wisdom for dealing with a failure in thrust in both engines was already codified in the QFH checklist, these steps could be tried quickly, which created the freedom to exercise creativity where it was needed.

Sully had studied other cases where there was no checklist. He knew about United Airlines Flight 232, where one engine failed, along with all three of the hydraulic systems that are necessary to control the plane — a billion-to-one chance occurrence. Captain Al Haynes and his crew brainstormed and experimented, and figured out that they could get some measure of control by varying the thrust of the two remaining engines. By doing so, they were able to pull off a crash landing. While one hundred people died, 185 survived because of their creativity.

Flight 1549's problem had no acceptable checklist either. What options could they consider? Landing at the nearby airports quickly seemed out of the question. As Sully put it, "Attempting to reach a runway that was unreachable could have catastrophic consequences for everyone on the airplane and who knows how many people on the ground."

Landing on a highway was another possibility, but wouldn't work here either: "If there had been a major interstate highway without overpasses, road signs, or heavy traffic, I could have considered landing on it." Nothing nearby fit that bill.

They needed a creative solution. A water landing? There were two options: Flushing Bay near La Guardia airport and the Hudson River.

Reasoning

Once you've gathered the information you need to make your decision, you draw conclusions from this information by using the superhabit of Reasoning. Reasoning is the habit of moving logically from one step to the next until you reach a conclusion. Sully practiced this superhabit frequently.

Pilots I have known who make it look the most effortless have something that goes beyond competence and beyond being someone who can be trusted. Such pilots seem able to find a well-reasoned solution to most every problem. They see flying as an intellectual challenge and embrace every hour in the sky as another learning opportunity. I've tried to be that kind of pilot. I've derived great satisfaction from becoming good at something that's difficult to do well.

This superhabit was vitally important that day.

I was judging what I saw out the window and creating, very quickly, a three-dimensional mental model of where we were. It was a conceptual and visual process, and I was doing this while flying the plane.

The conclusion that Sully derived from his reasoning was that a water landing was the right solution.

Even when you've collected the information you need, drawn conclusions from it, and come up with your decision, the work of Practical Wisdom is not yet done. The superhabit of Practical Wisdom is not complete until you've *acted on* your decision. A decision is not truly "made" until the decision is implemented — the plane has to be landed.

Successful implementation of a decision requires three things: keeping stock of the situation as it evolves, staying focused on your goals (and updating them when necessary), and anticipating and avoiding obstacles to implementation.

ALERTNESS

Alertness is the superhabit for having situational awareness. This can be developed by practicing paying attention to your surroundings and experiences. Sully was in the habit of doing this.

> Before I go to work, I build a "mental model" of my day's flying. I begin by creating that "situational awareness" so often stressed when I was in the Air Force. I want to know, before I even arrive at the airport, what the weather is like between where I am and where I'm going, especially if I'm flying across the continent.

Each time he took off from or landed at a new airport, he tried to "pay attention to the specific details of a place, and to hold on to a mental picture of the view. It could be helpful the next time I return, even if it's years later."

Sully's practice of Alertness — like any other superhabit — extended to all aspects of his life, and in this case enabled him to bring some more relevant information into play. He knew that even if he were able to land the plane on the water without damage, a "serious rescue effort" would be needed immediately. The life expectancy of someone immersed in a January-cold New York river can be as low as thirty minutes.

Years earlier, on a visit to the Sea-Air-Space Museum housed on the *USS Intrepid*, which is docked permanently on the Hudson River, he had "noticed there were a lot of maritime resources nearby … there would be ferries and other rescue boats close by, not to mention large contingents of the city's police and ambulance fleets just blocks away."

The Hudson River had the resources for that serious rescue effort.

FORESIGHT

Foresight is the superhabit for having the right goals, and updating them as necessary, as conditions change. The goals of Flight 1549 at takeoff were to bring passengers and plane safely and on time to their destination in Charlotte, North Carolina. The loss of both engines required a quick reprioritization of these goals. Now it was passenger safety first, and plane safety second. In fact, Sully realized that to achieve the first goal of passenger safety would mean that he would likely have to sacrifice the plane. (Getting to Charlotte would have to wait for another day; "on time" was out of the question.)

3:29:11 PM — 4 MINUTES 17 SECONDS SINCE TAKEOFF

He made an announcement to the passengers, his only one since the engine failures:

> "This is the Captain. Brace for impact."

A few seconds later he spoke to Air Traffic Control: "We're gonna be in the Hudson."

The controller had difficulty believing his ears. He tried to get clarification, but at this point Sully had to put all his concentration on these final and most dangerous seconds of the doomed flight.

PREPAREDNESS

Along with scouring your surroundings and prioritizing your goals, effective implementation of a decision also requires anticipating and preparing for problems. Prussian field marshal Helmuth von Moltke once wrote "No plan survives first contact with the enemy." Boxer Mike Tyson put it more graphically: "Everyone has a plan until they get punched in the mouth."

Preparedness is the superhabit for anticipating the obstacles you might hit in the process of implementing your decisions, and deciding what you will do to avoid them. If you are the kind of person to whom bad things often seem to happen, lack of preparedness may be the root cause. Growing in the superhabit of Preparedness will help.

Research suggests that Preparedness is associated with success in academic and workplace settings. It is also one of the most crucial factors in adapting to life stressors and natural disasters. Studies of victims of natural disasters, for example, suggest that individuals with higher Preparedness tend to withstand stressful times better.

Preparedness is the habit of thinking through the possibilities of what might go wrong and what you could do about it — before you get punched in the mouth. Flight 1549 had certainly taken a hit. However, like most airline pilots, Captain Sullenberger knew, at some level, that he needed to be prepared: "Every time we push back from the gate, we must be prepared for the unexpected."

He knew at this point that a water landing was the only option — and he was well aware of the dangers of such a landing. A 1996 attempted water landing of hijacked Ethiopian Airlines Flight 961, for example, ended in near disaster when one "wingtip struck the water first, and [the plane] spun violently and broke apart." Of the 175 people on board, 125 died from the impact or from drowning. (Those pilots had to contend with hijackers battling them for control of the airplane, which, fortunately, was one problem that Sully did not have.) He knew that the biggest dangers in the next few seconds were hitting the water unevenly or stalling, both of which could be catastrophic. He had to focus on keeping the plane level, and managing airspeed by manipulating the plane's pitch attitude.

3:30:43 PM — 5 MINUTES 49 SECONDS AFTER TAKEOFF

Less than six minutes after takeoff, and only three and a half minutes after the engine failures, the plane landed on the Hudson River. Immediately First Officer Skiles went through the evacuation checklist, and Sullenberger opened the cockpit door and calmly yelled "Evacuate."

Within minutes, the flight attendants had moved all the passengers onto the wings and into the emergency inflating rafts.

The river was freezing cold, with a serious risk of deadly hypothermia for anyone who fell in. Fortunately, nearby ferries and emergency personnel responded immediately to the shocking sight of a passenger airliner landing on their river, and rushed to the scene. Every single person on the flight was saved.

After reaching shore, there was a humorous moment when Sullenberger called the U.S. Airways Operations Control Center to check in with them. The duty operations manager picked up the phone and in a rushed voice said, "I can't talk right now. There's a plane down in the Hudson!" Uh, yeah.

To grow in Practical Wisdom, one can practice each of these eight superhabits separately, until each becomes second nature. For example, in an office setting, you can work at your own pace on an important strategic decision, exercising each of them deliberately to ensure the best decision outcome possible. But in a situation where you have seconds to make decisions, with 155 lives in your hands, as Sully did, then all eight superhabits must kick into action at the same time. This can only happen if you have already developed them. In Sully's words, "Flight 1549 wasn't just a five-minute journey. My entire life led me safely to that river."

Captain Sullenberger and the crew of Flight 1549 behaved heroically and were treated as the heroes that they are. The reactions of people to the incident are instructive. Sully wrote: "I have people coming up to me with tears in their eyes. They're not sure why they're crying. Their feelings about what the flight represents, and then the surprise of meeting me, just cause a swell of emotion."

What *does* Flight 1549 represent? Here's what I think. It is the coming together of competence and decency, of true human excellence. Human excellence means not just being supremely competent, being really good at what you do. It also means using that competence in the service of others. The pilots, the crew, and the first responders embodied both senses of the word "good": they were good at their jobs, and did good to others. The plane was landed safely and everyone was rescued.

This integration of both types of "good" is the very essence of virtue. It is an uplifting and inspiring thing to see. This, I believe, is what Flight 1549 stands for, and why its captain and crew earned such an overwhelming emotional response from people.

We usually think of competence and decency — effectiveness and ethics — as two separate things. We know that there are highly competent people who do evil things and that there are ethical people who are incompetent. Both make the world a worse place, in their own ways.

That's not the case with virtue. Self-Discipline, Courage, Practical Wisdom, and all the virtues — the superhabits — always make you *simultaneously* both more effective and ethical.

Think about it. Is Self-Discipline something that makes you more effective, or that makes you a better person? It's both. Always. It's always more effective to act with Self-Discipline than to be self-indulgent. And it's always morally better to be self-disciplined than to be self-indulgent.

Is it possible to make a bad use of a virtue? No. The full definition of a virtue is "a good habit of the mind, by which we live righteously, of which no one can make bad use." If you make a bad use of a virtue, or a superhabit, it is not a virtue or superhabit, by definition.

Remember, superhabits are not something foreign to you. They already exist within you, like unused muscles. You just need to start exercising them. But those "muscles" can only be used in certain ways. If you try to use them for something inappropriate, they won't work. It's like trying to use the muscles in your tongue to wind a wristwatch. It won't work. They're just not made that way. Likewise, superhabits cannot be used for evil — they're just not made that way.

Let's say that you are trying to cultivate the virtue of Courage, but you want to use it to rob a bank. You want to overcome the fear that would arise, naturally, if you held up a teller in broad daylight, and reframe it as a challenge, so that it will give you more energy to steal.

It won't work. You'd be trying to using those "muscles" for something they weren't designed for. What you're developing may *resemble* Courage. You might learn to proceed despite your fears of getting caught, or shot. But you're not building a superhabit. A superhabit doesn't just make your life easier, it also makes you happier and healthier. Practicing robbing banks will make it easier for you to rob banks, but you will not find yourself becoming calmer, healthier, or happier.

The word *virtue* is not commonly used in our world today. Indeed, for many people it's almost a "bad" word — as in "virtue signaling," which, according to the Urban Dictionary, means "To take a conspicuous but essentially useless action ostensibly to support a good cause but actually to show off how much more moral you are than everybody else." That doesn't make virtue sound very attractive.

This is why I've mostly used the word *superhabit* in this book. But the *idea* of virtue, properly understood as the unification of competence and decency, is beautiful. When we see someone displaying the height of competence for a good cause, like Captain Sullenberger and his crew, we are struck by it. We recognize its attractiveness, and we want it for ourselves.

If you build the superhabits in this book, quietly, year after year, as Sully did, you will find your life increasing in calm, joy, and strength. One day, you too might be in a position to help people in some dramatic way, and perhaps even to inspire millions. You will never know if, how, or when the moment will come, until it does. You just have to get ready.

The difference between virtue signaling and virtue is perhaps nowhere more evident than in our final superhabit, Justice. Like Courage (which governs our fears), Self-Discipline (which governs our desires), and Practical Wisdom (which governs our thoughts), Justice is also a cardinal superhabit. It governs our actions, so that at all times we act justly, giving others what is due to them.

#13

Justice

JOHN NEWTON WAS BORN in 1725. His early days were hard. His mother died when he was seven years old. When he was eleven, his father took him to sea. When he was eighteen, he was pressed into the Royal Navy. To be "pressed" was to be captured by a "press-gang" — the official "recruiters" for the Royal Navy — who grabbed innocent civilians and dragged them aboard ship to serve in the navy. This was a regular feature of life in England in the mid-1700s.

Newton hated life in the navy, and attempted to desert. He was caught, flogged, and then expelled from the navy and given to a passing slave-trading ship, in exchange for one of their sailors. He was disrespectful and disobedient to his new captain, and left this new ship to try a land-based slave-trading career on the coast of West Africa, but he was enslaved himself until eventually rescued by another slave-trading ship. Despite his first-hand experience of its gruesomeness, he found the slave trade to be "an easy and creditable way of life" and decided to stay with it.

A re-conversion in 1748 to the Christianity of his childhood didn't change these views, at least initially. In fact, he went on to become captain of a slave-trading ship and was an active participant in "tearing husbands away from their wives and children, shackling these screaming men in heavy fetters, and chaining them in horrific, overcrowded squalor that would have disgraced the animal pens of an abattoir."

After several years, illness led to him giving up this career. His sense of faith growing, he studied for the Anglican ministry and eventually was ordained.

In 1788, a full forty years after his religious conversion, he got involved in the campaign to abolish the slave trade, and published

Thoughts upon the African Slave Trade, in which he told, in graphic detail, the story of his earlier experiences and apologized for them. Did it take four decades for Newton to realize the atrocities he had been conducting? The conventional account is that he, like the vast majority of the people of his time, had been blind to this grave injustice. One biographer argues that Newton "can hardly be criticized for failing to trouble his conscience ... at a time when no one else was much troubled about the morality of trafficking in human slaves."

Did he just wake up one day, full of regret for what he had done forty years prior, and begin to campaign for abolition? That seems highly unlikely. Each of us knows from experience that we can change our minds quickly, but changing our habits and ways of living tends to take a lot longer. It takes ongoing practice to build new habits.

A recent and remarkable discovery by British historian Professor John Coffey sheds some light on when exactly Newton changed his mind about the slave trade. In 1762, twenty-six years before Newton published *Thoughts upon the African Slave Trade*, and only six years after his final voyage, an anonymous account was published in a book by an American Quaker, Anthony Benezet, about a slave trading voyage from Liverpool to West Africa. In this account, the author describes the terrible tortures inflicted on the captives and explicitly condemns the slave trade.

Professor Coffey, through careful analysis of the records of the thousands of slave trading voyages of that time, matches the description of the ship and its voyage with the one Newton was sailing on at exactly that time, and concludes, convincingly, that the author was none other than Newton himself. So Newton understood, much earlier than has been historically recognized, the gravity of the evil that he had been complicit in. The subsequent years and decades, then, were not about him coming slowly to that realization. Rather, they were about aligning his actions with his beliefs — about growing in the superhabit of Justice.

By all accounts, as a young man Newton was what we might today call "a real piece of work." He was dishonest, disrespectful, disobedient, unfriendly, and deeply ungrateful to those who tried to help him. A friend of his family gave him a job in a time of need, and he never showed up. He repaid the ship's captain who rescued him from his captivity on the African coast by disrespecting him and undermining his authority.

Justice, like the other cardinal virtues, has several connected superhabits. Honesty, Respect, Obedience, Friendliness, and Gratitude are some of them. Justice requires giving to every person what is owed to them: we owe truth to those we communicate with; we owe respect to those who are worthy of honor; we owe obedience to legitimate authority; we owe gratitude to those who have done good to us; and we even owe friendliness to those with whom we come in contact. No wonder that Newton was so uncomplainingly involved in such a viciously unjust trade — he was lacking in all the subordinate superhabits of Justice.

It is good to reflect on this: in order to grow in our ability to exercise Justice, we should try to make progress in the smaller, component superhabits. You are not likely to be successful in promoting Justice in the world if you are dishonest, disrespectful, and unfriendly in your daily life. Or, as Peterson's rule six says, "Set your house in perfect order before you criticize the world."

It took four decades of growth before Newton was strong enough in the superhabit of Justice to play an instrumental role in toppling the slave trade.

If you find that you have difficulty getting along with people, or building or maintaining relationships — or if you worry that you're not pulling your own weight, or behaving like the decent person you want to be — these are all indications that perhaps you should be working on one or more of the superhabits connected to Justice.

Our MECE analysis of the superhabit of Justice begins by recognizing two kinds of Justice: one-to-one, and many-to-one. "Commutative Justice" (from the word *commutation*, or "exchange") is for justice in any kind of one-to-one interaction, such as in commercial exchanges. "Distributive Justice" is for many-to-one justice, or what the community owes to each individual; we'll discuss that later in this chapter.

COMMUTATIVE JUSTICE

The superhabit of Commutative Justice is the habit of being fair in our commercial transactions, by paying or charging a fair price for what we buy or sell. Any kind of cheating, for example by disguising a material flaw in something we're selling, is a violation of Commutative Justice.

Friends of mine bought a house with a home office addition. After they bought the house, they found that the office was always cold (it was winter when they moved in). They removed the heating duct cover and underneath they found … nothing. There was no duct. The previous owner had stuck a duct cover on the wall, to pretend that the room was heated. Although you could argue that my friend — or his home inspector — should have done a better job at due diligence, there's no question that what the seller did was a violation of Commutative Justice.

If you grow in the superhabit of Commutative Justice and do business with others who do the same, then your transactions will be more efficient, because you won't have to keep double- and triple-checking each transaction to make sure that you're not getting cheated.

Newton began cultivating the superhabit of Commutative Justice in his first position after he left the slave trade. His appointment was as "surveyor of tides" in the port town of Liverpool. The job had nothing to do with surveying, and little to do with tides: he was a customs officer, responsible for ensuring that customs duties on imported goods were paid. Bribery was common in the "surveying" profession, frequently amounting to half of a surveyor's total income. Initially Newton went along with this practice. But after much reflection and discussion with trusted advisors, he decided to refuse all such "gratuities." He was growing in Justice.

One-to-one Justice can be further distinguished into superhabits for two different types of situations: equal situations and unequal situations. Equal situations are when what is owed can (at least theoretically) be repaid — for example, repaying a financial debt. Unequal situations are those where it is impossible to repay what is owed — for example, you can never fully repay your mother for giving you life.

There are two kinds of superhabits for equal situations: those that are strictly necessary, and those that aren't. Among those that are strictly necessary, there is one that is always strictly necessary, Honesty, because you should always be honest.

HONESTY

There is only one superhabit of Justice for equal situations that is always strictly necessary, the superhabit of Honesty. When we are communicating with others, we owe them the truth.

In discussing this virtue with my students, they quickly bring up examples where telling the truth could incur harm:

> "What if some creepy person stops me as I'm about to enter my home and asks me 'Do you live here?' Could I say, 'No, I'm just visiting a friend — who is a police officer and a mixed martial arts expert, with a large

gun collection'?" In other words, my students are asking whether you can lie to someone who demands the truth of you, if that truth will likely cause harm to yourself or another.

A classic example of this is the case of Sr. Simplice, the religious sister in Victor Hugo's masterpiece *Les Miserables*, who had never told a lie in her life. The hero of the novel, Jean Valjean, is on his way to save the poor orphan Cosette, and is hiding in the corner of a room where Sr. Simplice is praying. The misguided inspector Javert is searching for Valjean, and enters the room. He sees Sr. Simplice. He knew she had never lied in her life "and venerated her especially on account of it."

> "Sister," said he, "are you alone in this room?"
> There was a fearful instant ... The sister raised her eyes, and replied:
> "Yes."
> "Then," continued Javert, "excuse me if I persist — it is my duty — you have not seen this evening a person, a man — he has escaped and we are in search of him — Jean Valjean; you have not seen him?"
> The sister answered:
> "No."
> She lied. Two lies in succession, one upon another, without hesitation.

There is extensive philosophical debate about whether or not one should lie in extreme cases like this. For the purposes of growing in the superhabit of Honesty, these arguments about extreme cases are a distraction. We should leave them to the philosophers — especially because of the temptation to use them to justify lying in cases that are *not* extreme but merely uncomfortable.

Let's keep it simple. We should lie *as little as possible*. Honesty is crucial for both personal and societal well-being. Research indicates that lying is harmful to both your mental and physical health. One study followed a test group that was asked for the duration of the test not to tell any lies. The members were assessed weekly with a lie detector, and asked whether they had lied in the past week. Those who were able to refrain from lying had significantly better physical and mental health and improved personal relationships. Neuroscience research suggests that Honesty is a default mode and lying involves activating other networks, which can be more cognitively exhausting. Peterson's rule eight is paraphrased as "Tell the truth — or, at least, don't lie."

If you would like to grow in the superhabit of Honesty, here's a simple place to begin. Often we're tempted to fudge the truth when we don't know something we're asked, particularly when we think we should have known it. A useful tip, for when you're in that situation, is just to say, "I don't know." (I found this tip in what I thought was a delightful little book called *Swanson's Unwritten Rules*. I later found out that, ironically, Swanson had plagiarized most of his rules, including this one, from an earlier book, W. J. King's *Unwritten Laws of Engineering*.)

Or, as the ancient Chinese philosopher Confucius said, "Shall I teach you what knowledge is? When you know a thing, to hold that you know it; and when you do not know a thing, to allow that you do not know it — this is knowledge."

Remember that Honesty is a habit, and so like all other superhabits, anyone can acquire it. You just have to get started. Practicing saying, "I don't know" when you don't know is a good place to start.

Though Honesty is always necessary, there are two other superhabits of Justice for equal situations, Gratitude and Correction, that are only necessary in certain circumstances: when others have done something good, or bad, respectively.

Gratitude

When others have done good things to or for us, the appropriate response is the superhabit of Gratitude.

Gratitude is a real superpower. Extensive research links Gratitude with psychological, social, and physical benefits. Individuals who practice Gratitude tend to be happier, healthier, and have stronger interpersonal relationships. When people express Gratitude they experience feelings of joy and pleasure. Other research suggests that being grateful is associated with lower stress, improved quality of life, higher emotional awareness, as well as increased vitality, energy, and enthusiasm.

Attempts to increase Gratitude have been found to reduce physical and psychological symptoms, and increase overall well-being. One study showed that people who grew in Gratitude by keeping a daily Gratitude journal — writing down what they are grateful about — grew in both mental and physical health.

I tried this myself. While writing this book, I suffered from a bad case of sciatica. I had to stop writing, because the only position in which I was at all comfortable was lying flat on my back. I usually write at a stand-up desk, and I couldn't stand, or sit, for more than a few minutes at a time. I started a Gratitude journal — and now I'm pain free. Okay, I also did physical therapy, a (very) short course of oral steroids, and acupuncture. But I do think that the Gratitude journal has something to do with it, because some weeks later I stopped writing in my Gratitude journal, and the pain came back. Now I write in that journal every night!

Correction

Correction is the superhabit of issuing correction or punishment when others do bad things, and we are in authority over them, whether in an official law enforcement role, a supervisory role at work, or as a parent. It may seem odd to think of Correction as a superhabit, and part of the cardinal superhabit of Justice, that is, something that we "owe" to others. But failing to provide Correction (in respectful and appropriate ways, certainly) to those for whom we are responsible for can be quite harmful to them. Especially as a parent. Peterson's fifth rule is "Do not let your children do anything that makes you dislike them," and he lays out in convincing detail the tremendous harm that can come to children whose parents don't discipline them.

Honesty, Gratitude, and Correction are considered strictly necessary because they are called for in every case. The next two superhabits, Friendliness and Generosity, are habits for dealing with people and things, respectively. While both are superhabits, with the associated benefits of superhabits, neither is considered strictly necessary, in sense that Justice doesn't require you to be friendly or generous to every single person you encounter.

FRIENDLINESS

The superhabit for dealing with people is Friendliness. It is the habit of being friendly to those with whom you have interactions. See how it is "not strictly necessary": it would be impossible to try to be equally friendly to absolutely everyone whose path we cross.

As I've mentioned, I grew up on the island of Malta. It is a very small island. When I was growing up, it felt like everyone knew everyone. Years ago, my mother was walking one morning down the main street of the capital city, Valletta, with her friend Monica, who was visiting from England. Monica noticed that, as they walked along, every couple of minutes my mother would recognize some-one, wave at them, and say "Bye!" This bothered Monica, and at a certain point she said to my mother,

"I hope you don't mind my asking, but why do you say 'Bye' each time we pass one of your friends? It seems rude, as if you didn't want to talk to them."

"I never thought of that," my mother replied.

A couple of minutes later, she saw another of her friends.

"Hello!" she said, cheerfully.

"Hello!" this friend replied, somewhat surprised. The three of them stopped and had a pleasant conversation, lasting maybe five or seven minutes, and then they all continued walking.

"I see now why you say 'Bye,'" Monica said. "If we had to stop to talk to your friends each time we see one, it would take us the rest of the day to travel three blocks!"

For those of us who take public transportation, anonymity is a more common experience; we travel every day with a mass of strangers. Friendliness does not require that we walk through the entire subway car and introduce ourselves to every co-commuter. But if we start to notice the same person traveling in the same car every day, it would be a friendly thing to do to smile in recognition. If such encounters are reciprocated, it would be friendly to engage in conversation. Indeed, studies suggest that talking to strangers makes us happier.

Friendliness has a wide range of psychological benefits. Research in social psychology suggests that individuals who are friendly and kind tend to be happier, have more life satisfaction, and lower psychological distress. Friendliness is considered an important predictor of stronger relationships; it produces a greater number of social connections; and it leads to less relationship conflict.

John Newton was not a good friend in his younger days. When he was rescued from captivity in Africa, it turned out that the ship's captain who saved him was a friend of his father's. For that reason, the captain tried to befriend him. Newton responded by being disrespectful and mocking, even writing a song making fun of the captain, and teaching it to the entire crew.

Newton made dramatic progress in Friendliness in the years after he left the slave trade. As an Anglican minister, he spent a large amount of time visiting the families in his parish in Olney, Buckinghamshire, far more than the typical vicar spent. He and his wife were notable for their hospitality, hosting numerous visitors often for extended periods of time. One very long-staying visitor was the poet William Cowper, with whom Newton developed a lifelong friendship. This friendship endured through Cowper's serious struggles with depression, and indeed Cowper's survival through these struggles has been attributed to Newton's attention. He spent many hours each day and often late at night with Cowper.

GENEROSITY

The equivalent superhabit for dealing with *things* is Generosity, the habit of being willing to share what we have. Like Friendliness, it is not strictly necessary. It wouldn't make sense for me to give away everything I have, especially if I am responsible for supporting, say, a family or aging parents. Nevertheless, Generosity is a superpower, like all the other superhabits. As you practice Generosity, you'll experience improvements in your mood and increases in happiness, as well as reductions in depression and anxiety. Anyone can learn to grow in Generosity, by taking small, simple steps like spending some of your money on others.

After Newton gave up taking the bribes that came with his position as surveyor of tides, his income dropped by half. It dropped still further when he became an Anglican minister. Despite this, he cultivated the habit of Generosity. In Liverpool he made it a practice to try to help "the impoverished, the bereaved, and the sick" of his town, and he continued to do this once he moved to Olney. While he was there, a generous benefactor granted him an annual stipend more than three times his annual income; it appears that he spent most if not all of this on the poor of his parish and the upkeep of his church. A big change from buying and selling human beings for profit.

The rest of the superhabits of one-to-one Justice are for Justice in unequal situations. These are situations where, as we noted above, it is impossible to provide an equal return for what you have received. You can never adequately repay your mother for giving birth to you. You can be kind to her, help her when she needs help, even take her in and support her in her old age — but she gave you life, and you cannot give her life in return. Even if she were in some deadly danger, and you saved her life, you'd still only be giving her part of her life back. She gave you all of yours.

Even though it's impossible to pay what is due in full in such situations, it doesn't mean that you don't still "owe" something, as a matter of justice. There are several superhabits for handling these unequal situations. In increasing order of the difficulty of giving a fair return for what you have received, they are: Compliance, for what we owe to those in authority over us; Respect, for what we owe to those worthy of honor; Patriotism, for what we owe to our parents and our country, for giving us life and a place to live safely; and Religion for what we owe to God.

COMPLIANCE

Compliance, or Obedience, is the superhabit for obeying those in authority above us, such as our superiors at work, or those with legitimate governmental authority. Newton realized early on, even in his slave trading days, that this was a problem for him. When he was offered his first assignment as a ship's captain, he turned it down, preferring instead to sail as a first mate, recognizing that he should "learn to obey" before learning to command.

RESPECT

Respect is the superhabit of honoring the dignity of others. Research in hospital settings indicates that patients who feel respected by medical personnel report greater satisfaction with their care and improved clinical outcomes. Other studies show that feeling respected in the workplace is associated with employee job satisfaction, employee engagement, and decreased conflict. Similarly, students tend to be more engaged and successful in classes when teachers are respectful.

Curiously, this is the one superhabit where research shows the benefits to others, but the benefits to self haven't yet been studied, as best I can see. There is, however, research showing that if you do good to others you'll tend to become happier, and so it is reasonable to assume that in making others happy by respecting them, you will also make yourself happy.

PATRIOTISM

Patriotism is the superhabit of doing our duty to our parents and our country. Research on caring for one's parents suggests that it can help foster empathy, rebuild the family unit, and provide a sense of purpose. Studies also suggest that serving as a caretaker is associated with positive emotions, life satisfaction, and personal growth. Supporting one's country is linked to strong social bonds, increased trust, and compassion, and research in multiple countries on national pride has found that it is a predictor of overall well-being.

RELIGION

The superhabit of doing one's duty to God is quite a superpower, even measured just in terms of its this-worldly benefits. Research suggests that religion provides individuals with a sense of hope and is associated with positive impacts on mental health. Studies on mental health have found that religion is associated with reductions in suicidal ideation, drug abuse, anxiety, and depressive thoughts. Being religious is also linked to increases in optimism, self-esteem, purpose in life, and hope. It is also associated with improvements in cholesterol levels and eating habits and a reduction in risky sexual behaviors and cigarette smoking.

Individuals who are religious tend to have stronger interpersonal relationships and marital stability, as well as more social capital and social support. Furthermore, research suggests that being religious is a predictor of life satisfaction, subjective well-being, and functioning in all domains among both children and adults.

Studies suggest that one can become more religious or spiritual by praying, attending a congregation, engaging in charitable work, and practicing being compassionate. If you want to learn more about growing in the superhabit of Religion, a good place to start is to read Ross Douthat's excellent *New York Times* article "A Guide to Finding Faith" — and to try practicing what he suggests.

As an Anglican minister, one would expect Newton to practice the superhabit of Religion. This he began to do with great fervor, and even wrote a book of hymns, in collaboration with his friend Cowper, to honor God and serve their parishioners.

One of Newton's contributions to this book, *Olney Hymns*, has since become the "most sung, most recorded, and most loved hymn in the world," *Amazing Grace*.

> Amazing grace (how sweet the sound)
> That saved a wretch like me!
> I once was lost, but now am found,
> Was blind, but now I see.

DISTRIBUTIVE JUSTICE

The superhabit for justice from the community to the individual is Distributive Justice. Distributive Justice requires that those who are responsible for allocating shared benefits and burdens within any kind of organization or society do so fairly.

Research in social psychology suggests that Distributive Justice is perceived to be highest when rewards and costs are shared fairly in group settings. Studies also suggest that individuals tend to consider different allocation principles, such as merit, need, and equality, when engaging in distributive behavior in society.

Perceptions of distributive justice are associated with favorable attitudes in social settings, and the superhabit of Distributive Justice is linked to improved mood, life satisfaction, and empathy. On the contrary, when things are considered unfair and distributive justice is perceived to be low, individuals' emotions, cognition, and behavior can be negatively affected. Research in developmental psychology suggests that children tend to develop the concept of fairness and distributive justice at a young age. Distributive Justice can be improved in various settings (e.g., workplace, school, society, etc.) by emphasizing fairness and empathy within a group of people.

What counts as a fair distribution is debatable. Philosophers can, and do, argue vigorously about which principles to follow to ensure a just distribution of the benefits and burdens of living in society. The political process is where these arguments get worked out in practice.

By the late 1700s, a political movement against the slave trade had been building in Britain. Newton, whose guilt for his earlier participation in the slave trade never left him, became increasingly outspoken. By then, Newton had become famous because of his preaching, his *Olney Hymns*, and his other writings. So his was an important voice. The publication of his *Thoughts upon the African*

Slave Trade "was of vital importance in converting public opinion to the abolitionist cause."

Around this time, Newton befriended William Wilberforce, who was the son of a close acquaintance. Wilberforce had experienced a strong religious conversion himself, and sought out Newton for advice. He was thinking that he should become an Anglican minister, as Newton had. Newton advised him instead to remain in politics and work for justice.

Wilberforce took this to heart and became a major driving political force behind the abolition movement. Newton aided him by continuing to preach and write against the slave trade, and was invited to testify before various parliamentary committees.

Newton lived to see the fruits of these efforts. In 1807, just a few months before he died, the slave trade was abolished throughout the British Empire.

REASONABLENESS

There is one final superhabit of Justice that recognizes that sometimes you have to go beyond laws, rules, or customs in order to be truly just. It is the superhabit of Reasonableness. Aquinas gives the following example:

> The law requires deposits to be restored, because in the majority of cases this is just. Yet it happens sometimes to be injurious — for instance, if a madman were to put his sword in deposit, and demand its delivery while in a state of madness.... On these and like cases it is bad to follow the law, and it is good to set aside the letter of the law and to follow the dictates of justice and the common good.

The second rule of power of Stanford Business School professor Jeff Pfeffer (whom we met back in chapter 3) is "Break the rules." Pfeffer observes that rules are made by those in power, and not surprisingly tend to favor those in power. He cites research from warfare, sports, and business that shows how breaking rules allows the weak to triumph over the strong. When a rule is manifestly unjust, the virtuous thing to do may be to skirt or break it.

Legendary public-school teacher, author, and stand-up comedian Matthew Dicks puts it this way:

> If we want to make things happen, we sometimes need. . . . to break the rules, dodge regulation, defy the norms, and be daring. At work, I like to pilot the "I'm not going to do this — let's see what happens" plan. When a task seems arbitrary, meaningless, or purely bureaucratic, I try to avoid it at all costs, knowing that failure to execute it will almost certainly result in no trouble at all.

To be clear, rules are necessary for human beings to live together in peace. Anarchy is worse than living with less-than-ideal rules, so there is a high bar for deciding which rules to disregard, which rules or laws to consider unjust. Rev. Martin Luther King (citing Thomas Aquinas) described it this way: "Any law that uplifts human personality is just. Any law that degrades human personality is unjust." And, as King goes on to say, you must be willing to pay the price for breaking an unjust law:

> One who breaks an unjust law must do so openly, lovingly, and with a willingness to accept the penalty. I submit that an individual who breaks a law that conscience tells him is unjust, and who willingly accepts

the penalty of imprisonment in order to arouse the conscience of the community over its injustice, is in reality expressing the highest respect for law.

The superhabit of Reasonableness can be used to oppose anything from petty school bureaucrats to systemic injustice.

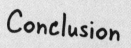

MAHALIA JACKSON WAS DEEPLY involved in the civil rights movement of the 1950s and 1960s. Her grandparents were born into slavery in Louisiana, and she grew up in poverty. She had an early passion for singing, and after moving with her family to Chicago, as part of the Great Migration North, her talent was recognized and she moved from success to success, becoming known as the "Queen of Gospel."

In 1947, she recorded a version of "Amazing Grace" that is now considered to be among the most notable. No doubt in part thanks to her, the hymn became the unofficial anthem of the civil rights movement.

In 1963, exactly two hundred years after Newton's anonymous exposé of the slave trade was published, Mahalia sang on the steps of the Lincoln Memorial to a crowd of a quarter of a million people gathered for the March on Washington. Shortly after she finished her last song, she stood by to watch her close friend Rev. Martin Luther King deliver the speech that was to be the grand finale of the day.

As she listened, she could tell that something was going very wrong. He was not achieving the resonance with his audience that he usually did — his words were falling flat, at this crucially important moment.

Inspired, Mahalia yelled,

> "Tell 'em about the dream, Martin, tell 'em about the dream!"

Reverend King had spoken of his dream of racial unity many times before, but that was not in this day's text. He paused, set aside his notes, and began to speak off the cuff:

I still have a dream.

It is a dream deeply rooted in the American dream. I have a dream that one day this nation will rise up and live out the true meaning of its creed: We hold these truths to be self-evident, that all men are created equal.

I have a dream that one day on the red hills of Georgia, the sons of former slaves and the sons of former slave owners will be able to sit down together at the table of brotherhood.

I have a dream that one day even the state of Mississippi, a state sweltering with the heat of injustice, sweltering with the heat of oppression will be transformed into an oasis of freedom and justice.

I have a dream that my four little children will one day live in a nation where they will not be judged by the color of their skin but by the content of their character.

This most famous part of King's celebrated speech, indeed arguably the part that made the entire event so memorable, was never in his speaking notes. It was all delivered spontaneously, in response to Mahalia's cry.

King wanted his children to be judged not by the color of their skin, but by the "content of their character." What is the content of your character? The content of our character, the ancients tell us, is the virtues — the superhabits.

How do we build these superhabits? Captain Sullenberger, the hero of Flight 1549, observed that:

Through the media, we all have heard about ordinary people who find themselves in extraordinary situations. They act courageously or responsibly, and their efforts are described as if they opted to act that way on the spur of the moment.... I believe many people in those situations actually have made decisions years before. Somewhere along the line, they came to define the sort of person they wanted to be, and then they conducted their lives accordingly.

Somewhere along the line, you must decide that you want to live your fullest life — a life of calm, joy, and strength. If and when you do, you will start to take the small repeated steps to build the superhabits that will give you this life.

The most important thing I want you to take away from this book is that the superhabits you have just read about are *not* optional strengths that could improve your life, or tools that you could add to your toolkit, but that you could reasonably do without. They are the necessary ingredients, the essential habits, for having a happy, healthy, and successful life. Ancient wisdom knew this. Modern science confirms it. The superhabits are muscles that you already have, which you need to build up in order to reach your potential. They are the content of your character.

A recent article from global consulting firm McKinsey & Company asks, "If we're all so busy, why isn't anything getting done?" The answer given is that we need to collaborate better. But in order to do so, we also need to get better at making decisions and dealing with our emotions, both our fears and our desires. The cardinal virtues of Justice, Practical Wisdom, Courage, and Self-Discipline, built through all their associated superhabits, are the habits we need to drive a total transformation in our lives, in our organizations, and in our societies.

As you've seen throughout this book, you should begin by choosing one superhabit and starting to practice it. The superhabits in this book are in a deliberate order, so the first one you came across that made you think "If this were a habit of mine, my life would be so much better" — *that's* the one you should start with. I've suggested a few simple first steps in this book. But there are also more listed on our website, superhabit.substack.com.

Don't just focus on your own growth. If you work in a team, or run an organization, encourage your colleagues to grow in superhabits too. You can survey your colleagues to identify your team's biggest superhabit gaps, and then work together to select one and begin practicing it. Superhabits are contagious. It should not be surprising to find that people working together tend to have similar superhabit strengths and superhabit gaps — and when some people grow in a superhabit, they will help others to improve in it as well.

As the members of your organization grow together, your organization's productivity should improve. Why shouldn't it? If everyone in the organization starts to become better at decision making, collaborating, and managing their emotions, your organization's performance should soar.

Best of all, regardless of organizational outcomes, everyone who begins growing in the system of superhabits will be on the path to an easier, happier, and healthier life.

Acknowledgements

I EXERCISE HERE THE superhabit of Gratitude toward the many people from whom I have learned so much about the virtue tradition.

At the founding of our business school in 2012, I invited colleagues from our School of Philosophy to give a series of lectures to our faculty, in order to help establish our school on a solid philosophical foundation. Lectures in this series by Msgr. Sokolowski (and subsequent conversations with him), and by Prof. (now Dean of Philosophy) Brad Lewis, along with one by Dr. Bob Kennedy from the University of St. Thomas in Minnesota at an inaugural conference for our new school, launched my interest in this topic.

That interest was furthered by books by my predecessor department chair, the late Dr. Alberto Piedra, by my colleague Dr. Michael Pakaluk, and by Jean-Francois Orsini and Alexandre Havard, and by several conversations with Dr. Russ Hittinger over the years.

My virtues as superhabits journey really began to get traction when my longtime colleague, friend, and co-editor Prof. (now Dean of Theology) Joe Capizzi recommended that I read Fr. Romanus Cessario's book *The Virtues, or the Examined Life*. This book, along with a couple of delightful dinners with its author, was my guide to a better understanding of Aquinas's *Treatise on the Virtues*.

An insightful comment by Laura Cermak during a lecture of mine, sharing an insight from Dr. John Cuddeback of Christendom College, about how the cardinal virtues each perfect different parts of the soul, turned out to be pivotal to my entire project.

My research assistants Zane Zieglar, Zohaib Jessani, and Cristina Batt plowed through the mountains of business biographies, positive psychology studies, and wisdom literature sources respectively, producing what became the raw material for this book, and Teresa Ryland's proficiency in Medieval Latin ensured that I did not misunderstand Aquinas.

Jonathan Bronitsky had many helpful suggestions about earlier drafts of the book.

John Bursch encouraged me to leave behind the "family tree" approach to the Anatomy of Virtue, which led to my developing the far superior "wheel" diagram, and Rob Headrick faithfully drew and redrew some dozen different iterations of the wheel.

I am grateful to Provost Roger Nutt and Ave Maria University for hosting me during what turned out to be the most important writing days in this project, to Fr. Paul Scalia for his ongoing advice and encouragement, and to Legatus chapters around the country and Thomistic Institute chapters at Yale University and elsewhere, over the past few years, for giving me the opportunity to work the ideas in this book out in discussion with intelligent and engaging audiences.

I am especially indebted to Dr. Melissa Moschella, Dr. Chris Blum, and Edward Hadas for reading earlier versions of the entire manuscript and providing lots of helpful suggestions, and to Austin Ruse for his enthusiastic encouragement – and introduction to his publisher.

All their help was invaluable in writing this book. Needless to say, any errors and/or idiosyncratic interpretations of Thomas Aquinas and the social science research are entirely my own.

I am grateful to the exceptional team at Sophia Institute Press, who are delightful to work with.

My six children and son-in-law each contributed their enthusiasm, questions, and insight. My two youngest daughters are also responsible for the distinctive color scheme of the Anatomy diagram.

My wife Kathleen, graduate of Thomas Aquinas College, first fed my love for Aquinas. This book benefited greatly from her constant support and fearless criticism. Indeed, I am quite sure that without her, it (not to mention our six children) would never have come into existence. To her, the love of my life, I dedicate this book.

Appendix

THE FINAL SEVEN SUPERHABITS are those for your intellectual and spiritual life. Since this book has focused largely on the practical contributions of superhabits, we haven't explored these much. For completeness' sake, though, I wanted to include at least a description of each here. (They actually deserve a whole book to themselves).

The superhabits of the intellectual life are the habits of knowledge — especially, but not exclusively, more abstract knowledge. They are Science, Art, Wisdom, and Understanding. Science is the superhabit of knowing the causes of things, how one thing causes another. Art is the superhabit of knowing how to make things. Understanding is the superhabit of knowing the first principles that underlie all of reality. Wisdom is the superhabit of understanding the highest causes of things.

The final three superhabits are those for the spiritual life. A recent Pew survey found that 83 percent of all U.S. adults believe that people have a soul or spirit in addition to their physical body. Aquinas certainly believed in the spiritual side of life. He was, after all, a Christian monk. While the earliest virtue traditions were philosophical, not religious, many of the world's major religions have incorporated a virtue tradition as well. Christianity, Judaism, Islam, Hinduism, Confucianism, Taoism, and Buddhism all have virtue traditions. With some small differences, they tend to include many of the same virtues we have been discussing here.

In Aquinas's system, he lists the spiritual (or theological) habits of Faith, Hope, and Love. Faith is the superhabit of believing in God. Hope is the superhabit of trusting in God to get you to Heaven. Love is the superhabit where we become united with God, and we wish for and do good for others. Many, if not most, religions teach that living this loving way is the highest and most noble form of human existence. As the apostle Paul wrote, "So faith, hope, love abide, these three; but the greatest of these is love" (1 Cor. 13:13).

Endnotes

INTRODUCTION

5   **the Peruvian city of Cusco:** "Cuzco, Peru, Once Capital of Incas, Is Scene of Panic; Death Toll May Rise: 50 Dead as Quake Hits Ancient City," *The Washington Post (1923-1954)*, 1950; George E. Ericksen, Jaime Fernández Concha, and Enrique Silgado, "The Cusco, Peru, Earthquake of May 21, 1950," *Bulletin of the Seismological Society of America* 44, no. 2A (1954): 97–112.

5   **builders had developed earthquake-proof construction techniques:** M. A. Rodríguez-Pascua, C. Benavente Escobar, L. Rosell Guevara et al., "Did Earthquakes Strike Machu Picchu?" *Journal of Seismology* 24, 883–895 (2020): 886, https://doi.org/10.1007/s10950-019-09877-4.

5   **earthquake-resistant structures:** Adele Peters, "Ancient Incans Earthquake Proof Walls Inspire These 3-D Printed Modern Structures," *Fast Company*, October 20, 2014, https://www.fastcompany.com/3037227/ancient-incans-earthquake-proof-walls-inspire-these-3-d-printed-modern-structures.

5   **allows modern buildings to resist earthquakes:** "Earthquake-Resistant House 3D Printed in Just 26 Hours" (2023), *New Atlas* https://newatlas.com/architecture/progreso-3d-printed-house/

6   ***Start with Why,*** **have** ***Grit,*** **have** ***Drive:*** Simon Sinek, *Start with Why: How Great Leaders Inspire Everyone to Take Action* (New York: Portfolio, 2009); Angela Duckworth, *Grit: The Power of Passion and Perseverance* (Toronto: Collins, 2018); Daniel Pink, *Drive: The Surprising Truth about What Motivates Us* (New York: Riverhead Books, 2009); Carol Dweck, *Mindset: Changing the Way You Think to Fulfill Your Potential* (London: Robinson, 2017); Brené Brown, *Daring Greatly: How the Courage to Be Vulnerable Transforms the Way We Live, Love, Parent, and Lead* (London: Penguin Random House, 2018); Jen Sincero, *You Are a Badass Every Day: How to Keep Your Motivation Strong, Your Vibe High, and Your Quest for Transformation Unstoppable* (New York: Viking, 2018); Susan Cain, *Quiet: The Power of Introverts in a World That Can't Stop Speaking* (Thorndike,

ME: Center Point, 2012); David J. Schwartz, *The Magic of Thinking Big* (New York: Penguin, 2014); Owain Service and Rory Gallagher, *Think Small* (London: Michael O'Mara Books, 2017); Gary Keller and Jay Papasan, *The ONE Thing* (Portland, OR: Bard Press, 2013); Mark Manson, *The Subtle Art of Not Giving a F*ck: A Counterintuitive Approach to Living a Good Life* (New York: Harperluxe, 2018).

7   **"distinct elements of talent"**: Marco Dondi et al., "Defining the Skills Citizens Will Need in the Future World of Work," McKinsey & Company, June 25, 2021, https://www.mckinsey.com/industries/ public-sector/our-insights/defining-the-skills-citizens-will-need-in-the-future-world-of-work#/.

7   **"capabilities"**: John Hagel, John Seely Brown, and Maggie Wooll, "Skills Change, but Capabilities Endure," Deloitte Insights, 2019, https://www2.deloitte.com/content/dam/insights/us/ articles/6332_From-skills-to-capabilities/6332_Skills-change-capabiliites-endure.pdf.

7   **"durable skills"**: Lauren Cole et al. "The High Demand for Durable Skills," America Succeeds, October 2021, https://americasucceed. wpengine.com/portfolio/the-high-demand-for-durable-skills-october-2021; "Developmental Assets Framework," Search Institute, https://searchinstitute.org/resources-hub/developmental-assets-framework.

7   **"character strengths"**: See C. Peterson and M. E. P. Seligman, *Character Strengths and Virtues: A Handbook and Classification* (Oxford: Oxford University Press, 2004).

7   **The Optimal Work project:** "Program Overview," The Human Flourishing Program at Harvard's Institute for Quantitative Social Science, Harvard University, https://hfh.fas.harvard.edu/about; "About," Michigan Ross Center for Positive Organizations, University of Michigan, https://positiveorgs.bus.umich.edu/about/; OptimalWork, www.optimalwork.com.

7   **Professors at Oxford University:** See Jonathan Brant, Edward Brooks, and Michael Lamb, eds., *Cultivating Virtue in the University* (Oxford: Oxford University Press, 2022).

7   **Classically, they are called *virtues*:** *Summa Theologiae*, I-II, q. 55, art. 1.

7   **they are like superpowers:** The word *superhabit*, throughout the book, always means the same thing as *virtue* in the classical sense. The reason I avoid using the word *virtue* is that it means so many different things to different people. But if you like the word, and understand it in its classical sense, feel free to substitute it in your mind every time you read the word *superhabit*.

8   **In this book I will introduce you to his system:** In addition to Aquinas's clear and comprehensive taxonomy, I will also draw from contemporary Thomistic scholarship, including that of Josef Pieper and Romanus Cessario, as well as also popular works in the virtue tradition, such as those by Romano Guardini, William Bennet, John Garvey, and Donald DeMarco.

8   **contemporary "habits" literature:** Charles Duhigg, *The Power of Habit: Why We Do What We Do in Life and Business* (New York: Random House, 2012); James Clear, *Atomic Habits* (New York: Penguin Random House, 2018); B. J. Fogg, *Tiny Habits: The Small Changes That Change Everything* (Boston: Houghton Mifflin, 2020).

8   **the "rules" literature:** Jordan Peterson, *12 Rules for Life: An Antidote to Chaos* (Toronto: Random House Canada, 2018); and *Beyond Order: 12 More Rules for Life* (New York: Portfolio/Penguin Random House, 2021); Jeffrey Pfeffer, *7 Rules of Power* (New York: Matt Holt Books, 2022).

8   **superhabits that become second nature:** There is also a fourth stream, the contemporary virtues literature with books by William Bennett, Romano Guardini, Donald DeMarco, John Garvey, and others.

9   **a recent Gallup survey:** *Alumni Experiences and Outcomes: The Busch School of Business at The Catholic University of America*, Gallup, 2021, https://communications.catholic.edu/news/2021/12/catholicuniversity_report_120621v2.pdf.

CHAPTER 1: RESTRAINT

14   **"Good Friday Agreement"**: Niall Kiely, "From the Archives: The Women for Peace Movement," *Irish Times*, August 11, 1976, https://www.irishtimes.com/opinion/august-11th-1976-1.594923; "A Woman of Peace," *The Scotsman*, July 28, 2006, https://www.scotsman.com/news/people/a-woman-of-peace-2465464; Judith Cummings, "'Troubles Became a Rallying Cry," BBC News, March 11, 2009, http://news.bbc.co.uk/2/hi/uk_news/northern_ireland/7937484. stm; "About the Good Friday Agreement," Department of Foreign Affairs, Ireland, https://www.ireland.ie/en/dfa/role-policies/northern-ireland/about-the-good-friday-agreement/.

14   **Restraint:** Thomas Aquinas uses the word *continentia*, which is usually translated as "continence." That word today makes many people think of bladder control. We will run into the problem of the changed meanings of the English translations of Latin names of virtues time and again. In each case, for alternative translations I have referred to Roy Joseph Deferrari, *A Latin-English Dictionary of St. Thomas Aquinas: Based on the Summa Theologica and Selected Passages of His Other Works* (Boston: St. Paul, 1960). Dr. Deferrari was an earlier predecessor of mine as provost at Catholic University. In this case, for *continentia* he also gives "Restraint," which I have used here.

14   **people who have developed the habit of Restraint:** R. F. Baumeister and J. M. Tierney, *Willpower: Rediscovering the Greatest Human Strength* (New York: Penguin, 2012).

14   **higher grades, better school attendance:** J. P. Tangney, A. L. Boone, and R. F. Baumeister, "High Self-Control Predicts Good Adjustment, Less Pathology, Better Grades, and Interpersonal Success," *Self-Regulation and Self-Control* (2018): 173–212, https://doi.org/10.4324/9781315175775-5.

14   **short- and long-term happiness and life satisfaction:** W. Hofmann et al., "Yes, but Are They Happy? Effects of Trait Self-Control on Affective Well-Being and Life Satisfaction," *Journal of Personality* 82, no. 4 (August 2014): 265–277. https://doi.org/10.1111/jopy.12050.

15 **greater financial security:** T. E. Moffitt et al., "A Gradient of Childhood Self-Control Predicts Health, Wealth, and Public Safety," *Proceedings of the National Academy of Sciences* 108, no. 7 (2011): 2693–2698, https://doi.org/10.1073/pnas.1010076108.

16 **a reduction in depression, anxiety, and chronic pain:** M. Ng, and W. Wong, "The Differential Effects of Gratitude and Sleep on Psychological Distress in Patients with Chronic Pain," *Journal of Health Psychology*, 18, no. 2 (2012): 263–271, https://doi.org/10.1177/1359105312439733.

17 **Dewey was the childhood name of Dwayne Johnson:** Chris Health, "Dwane Johnson Lets Down His Guard," *Vanity Fair*, November 2021, https://www.vanityfair.com/hollywood/2021/10/dwayne-johnson-speaks-his-truth; Shuvangi Sen Chaudhury, "'Always F****ng Angry': Dwayne Johnson Opens Up on His Regular Arrests at Age 15," *Essentially Sports*, April 25, 2022, https://www.essentiallysports.com/wwe-news-always-fng-angry-dwayne-johnson-opens-up-on-his-regular-arrests-at-age-15-the-rock/; Akash Dhakite, "Dwayne 'The Rock' Johnson Looks Back at the Hardships He and His Parents Faced during the 80s: 'You Can See It in Their Faces,'" *Essentially Sports*, March 17, 2022, https://www.essentiallysports.com/wwe-news-dwayne-the-rock-johnson-looks-back-at-the-hardships-he-and-his-parents-faced-during-the-80s-you-can-see-it-in-their-faces/; "How a High School Coach Changed Dwayne Johnson's Life," *Oprah*, season 5, episode 504, November 15, 2015, https://www.oprah.com/own-master-class/how-a-high-school-coach-changed-dwayne-johnsons-life-video; Jade Scipioni, "Dwayne 'The Rock' Johnson on Where He Gets His Drive: 'I Didn't Want to Be Evicted Anymore'" CNBC Make It, January 12, 2021, https://www.cnbc.com/2021/01/12/dwayne-the-rock-johnson-on-where-he-gets-his-drive.html; Christopher Hooton, "Literally Just 3 Minutes with Dwayne 'The Rock' Johnson, the Biggest Movie Star on the Planet" *Independent*, April 17, 2018, https://www.independent.co.uk/arts-entertainment/films/features/dwayne-johnson-interview-the-rock-rampage-film-meditation-future-a8308946.html.

18 **not simply an improvement in the task at hand:** Roy F. Baumeister et al., "Self-Regulation and Personality: How

Interventions Increase Regulatory Success, and How Depletion Moderates the Effects of Traits on Behavior," *Journal of Personality* 74, no. 6 (December 2006): 1773–1801. doi.org/10.1111/j. 1467-6494.2006.00428.x.

18   **They collected volunteers from a meditation seminar:** M. Friese, C. Messner, and Y. Schaffner, "Mindfulness Meditation Counteracts Self-Control Depletion," *Consciousness and Cognition* 21, no. 2 (June 2012): 1016–1022, https://doi.org/10.1016/j.concog.2012.01.008; M. S. Hagger et al., "Ego Depletion and the Strength Model of Self-Control: A Meta-analysis," *Psychological Bulletin*, 136, no. 4 (2010): 495–525, https://doi.org/10.1037/a0019486.

CHAPTER 2: HUMILITY

23   **"a really big idea":** Sara Randazzo, "The Elizabeth Holmes Trial: Founder Recounts 'Big Idea' That Led to Creation of Theranos," *Wall Street Journal*, November 22, 2021, https://www.wsj.com/articles/the-elizabeth-holmes-trial-founder-recounts-big-idea-that-led-to-creation-of-theranos-11637616327.

23   **affirmations about herself:** Sara Randazzo, "Elizabeth Holmes and 'Sunny' Balwani's Handwritten Notes Detailed How to Live," *Wall Street Journal*, December 2, 2021, https://www.wsj.com/articles/elizabeth-holmes-and-sunny-balwanis-handwritten-notes-detailed-how-to-live-11638480502?mod=ig_theranoscoverage.

24   **"a culture of isolation, secrecy, retaliation and fear":** Heather Somerville, "In Elizabeth Holmes Trial, Ex-Theranos Employees Cite Culture of Fear and Isolation," *Wall Street Journal*, November 13, 2021, https://www.wsj.com/articles/in-elizabeth-holmes-trial-ex-theranos-employees-cite-culture-of-fear-and-isolation-11636812000.

24   **a jail sentence for Holmes for fraud:** Chantal Da Silva, "Disgraced Theranos Founder Elizabeth Holmes' Prison Sentence Shortened by 2 Years," NBC News, July 11, 2023, https://www.nbcnews.com/news/us-news/disgraced-theranos-founder-elizabeth-holmes-prison-sentence-appears-sh-rcna93593.

24   **"If you undertake some role":** Epictetus, *Handbook*, 37.

25 **"more good people need to have power":** Pfeffer, *7 Rules of Power,* xi.

25 **"building a positive relationship":** Pfeffer, *7 Rules of Power,* 19–20.

25 **"accomplished, successful people":** Pfeffer, *7 Rules of Power,* 21.

26 **to be able to design the best cathedral in the world:** C.S. Lewis, *The Screwtape Letters* (London: William Collins, 2012).

27 **one of Wall Street's top thought leaders:** Jason DeSena Trennert, *My Side of the Street* (New York: St. Martin's Press, 2015), 93 and 99.

27 **less relationship conflict, and lower stress:** D.E. Davis et al., "Humility and the Development and Repair of Social Bonds: Two Longitudinal Studies," *Self and Identity,* 12, no. 1 (2012): 58–77; N. Krause, "Religious Involvement, Humility, and Change in Self-Rated Health over Time," *Journal of Psychology and Theology,* 40, no. 3 (2012): 199–210, https://doi.org/10.1177/009164711204000303; Jennifer Cole Wright et al., "The Psychological Significance of Humility," *Journal of Positive Psychology* 12, no. 1 (2017):, 3–12, doi. org/10.1080/17439760.2016.1167940.

27 **humble CEOs get better results:** A.Y. Ou, D.A. Waldman, and S.J. Peterson, "Do Humble CEOs Matter? An Examination of CEO Humility and Firm Outcomes," *Journal of Management,* 44, no. 3 (2018): 1147–1173, https://doi.org/10.1177/0149206315604187. One study suggests, however, that these results arise not because of actual better performance, but because analysts have lower expectations for their firms: O.V. Petrenko et al., "The Case for Humble Expectations: CEO Humility and Market Performance," *Strategic Management Journal* 40, no. 12 (December 2019): 1938–1964. https://doi.org/10.1002/smj.3071.

27 **Entrepreneur Kim Landi:** Christina Desmarais, "33 Daily Habits Highly Successful People Have (and the Rest of Us Probably Don't)," Inc., December 21, 2017, https://www.inc.com/christina-desmarais/33-things-highly-successful-people-are-doing-every-day-that-you-probably-arent.html.

28   "Many young businesspeople feel that minor chores are beneath their dignity": W. J. King, *The Unwritten Laws of Business* (New York: Currency, 2007), 5.

29   without even having to think about it: Aristotle describes the stages from vice to virtue as vice, incontinence, continence, and virtue. Again, given the contemporary understanding of the word *continence* (*Merriam-Webster*: the ability to retain a bodily discharge voluntarily, https://www.merriam-webster.com/dictionary/continence), I have instead adopted the popular and helpful Four Stages of Competence model from Frank Anthony DePhillips, William M. Berliner, and James J. Cribbin, "Meaning of Learning and Knowledge," *Management of Training Programs* (Homewood, IL: Richard D. Irwin, 1960), 69, https://archive.org/details/managementoftrai0000deph/page/n1/mode/2up.

29   a workbook to help you grow: Caroline R. Lavelock, Everett L. Worthington, Jr., and Don E. Davis, *The Path to Humility: Six Practical Sections for Becoming a More Humble Person*, https://evworthington.squarespace.com/s/the-path-to-humility-six-practical-sections-for-becoming-a-more-humble-person.pdf.

30   (which you do): Although scholars still debate this, there is evidence that aspects of intelligence can by improved through various exercises. See e.g., Robert J. Sternberg, "Increasing Fluid Intelligence Is Possible after All," *Proceedings of the National Academy of Sciences* 105, no. 19 (2008): 6791–6792; and Susanne M. Jaeggi et al., "Improving Fluid Intelligence with Training on Working Memory," *Proceedings of the National Academy of Sciences* 105, no. 19 (2008): 6829–6833, https://www.pnas.org/doi/abs/10.1073/pnas.0801268105; but see also Richard J. Haier, "Increased Intelligence Is a Myth (So Far)," *Frontiers in Systems Neuroscience* 8, no. 34 (2014), https://www.ncbi.nlm.nih.gov/pmc/articles/PMC3950413/ and Lazar Stankov and Jihyun Lee, "We Can Boost IQ: Revisiting Kvashchev's Experiment," *Journal of Intelligence* 8, no. 4 (2020): 41, https://pubmed.ncbi.nlm.nih.gov/33256082/.

30   Writing down what you don't know will help your humility: Elizabeth J. Krumrei-Mancuso and Malika Rice Begin, "Cultivating Intellectual Humility in Leaders: Potential Benefits, Risks, and

Practical Tools," *American Journal of Health Promotion* 36, no. 8 (2022): 1404–1411.

CHAPTER 3: DILIGENCE

33 **"You did something and something happened":** Carly Fiorina, *Tough Choices: A Memoir* (New York: Portfolio, 2006), 19.

33 **first woman ever to become CEO of a Fortune 20 company:** Fiorina, *Tough Choices*, chap. 3.

34 **that's how some dictionaries define it:** See *Merriam-Webster*, s.v. "diligence," accessed July 8, 2024, https://www.merriam-webster.com/dictionary/diligence.

34 **diligence is about intense study driven by a love of knowing:** Following Deferrari (*A Latin-English Dictionary*), I am translating *studiositas* (II-II, q. 166) as "Diligence." "Studiousness" just does not do justice to *studiositas*. As Pieper argues: "It would be easy enough to render [*studiositas* and its opposing vice, *curiositas*], following the dictionary, as 'desire for knowledge,' or 'zeal,' for the first, and 'inquisitiveness' for the second. But this would amount to suppressing their most important meaning … *Studiositas, curiositas* — by these are meant temperateness and intemperance, respectively, in the natural striving for knowledge, temperateness and intemperance, above all, in the indulgence of the sensual perception of the manifold sensuous beauty of the world; temperateness and intemperance in the 'desire for knowledge and experience.' " Josef Pieper, *The Four Cardinal Virtues* (Notre Dame, IN: University of Notre Dame Press, 1966), 198. Admittedly, "diligence" carries this broader meaning with some difficulty. But it works and I have not found a better word.

34 **"intelligence can only be led by desire":** Simone Weil, *Waiting for God*, cited in John H. Garvey, *The Virtues* (Washington, D.C.: The Catholic University of America Press, 2022), 117.

35 **he had trouble staying awake:** R. G. LeTourneau, *Mover of Men and Mountains* (Chicago: Moody, 1972), 54.

35 **"I had a one-man graduation ceremony for myself":** Ibid.

36 **Diligence is associated with better GPA:** H. Bernard, J.D. Thayer, and E. A. Streeter, "Diligence and Academic Performance," *Journal of Research on Christian Education* 2, no. 2 (1993), 213–234, https://doi.org/10.1080/10656219309484785; B. M. Galla et al., "The Academic Diligence Task (ADT): Assessing Individual Differences in Effort on Tedious but Important Schoolwork," *Contemporary Educational Psychology*, 39, no. 4 (October 2014): 314–325, https://doi.org/10.1016/j.cedpsych.2014.08.001; P. H. Oliver, D. W. Guerin, and A. W. Gottfried, "Temperamental Task Orientation: Relation to High School and College Educational Accomplishments," *Learning and Individual Differences* 17, no. 3 (2007): 220–230, https://doi.org/10.1016/j.lindif.2007.05.004.

36 **ways in which you might be *wasting* this valuable desire:** The following three unproductive uses of the desire to know things are based on Aquinas, *Summa Theologica* II-II, q. 167 and Pieper, *The Four Cardinal Virtues*, 199–202.

36 **two and a half hours each day:** Simon Kemp, "Digital 2023 Deep Dive: How Much Time Do We Spend on Social Media?," DataReportal, January 26, 2023, https://datareportal.com/reports/digital-2023-deep-dive-time-spent-on-social-media#.

36 *flow:* M. Csikszentmihalyi, *Flow: The Psychology of Optimal Experience* (New York: Harper & Row, 1990).

37 **When their skill level matched ... they experienced flow:** C. J. Fullagar, P. A. Knight, and H. S. Sovern, "Challenge/Skill Balance, Flow, and Performance Anxiety," *Applied Psychology* 62, no. 2 (April 2013): 236–259, https://doi.org/10.1111/j.1464-0597.2012.00494.x.

37 **psychiatric institution:** Kris Lee, "The Imaginary Engineeer: Karl Hans Janke's Flights of Fancy," *Cabinet* 29 (Spring 2008), https://www.cabinetmagazine.org/issues/29/lee.php.

37 **false or unreliable information:** Aquinas identifies interest in the occult here, which is why the Oliver Lodge example is particularly apt, I think. *Summa Theologica* II-II, q. 167, art. 1.

38 **Marconi's discoveries led to immense practical benefits:** For a fascinating account of the race between Marconi and Lodge, made even more readable by being incorporated into a true-life murder story, read Eric Larson, *Thunderstruck* (New York: Broadway Books, 2006).

38 **ended up studying more themselves:** N. Mehta, R. Stinebrickner, and T. Stinebrickner, *Time-Use and Academic Peer Effects in College* (Cambridge, MA: National Bureau of Economic Research, 2018), https://doi.org/10.3386/w25168.

39 **the process of cultivating interest is intrinsically rewarding:** K. A. Renninger and S. E. Hidi, "To Level the Playing Field, Develop Interest," *Policy Insights from the Behavioral and Brain Sciences* 7, no. 1 (2020): 10–18, https://doi.org/10.1177/2372732219864705.

39 **three research-based ideas:** Questions derived from ibid.

39 **rather than trying to force them with your willpower:** Not all virtue traditions hold this view of the role of the emotions. There is a (centuries-) long debate, initially between the Stoics and the Peripatetics, on this topic.

CHAPTER 4: HABITS VS. SUPERHABITS

44 **Thompson had a punishing daily regimen:** Jon Hendershott, "T&FN Interview: Daley Thompson," *Track and Field News* (April 1984): 4042, https://trackandfieldnews.com/wp-content/uploads/2019/01/daley-thompson.pdf.

44 **You have to be outstanding in all ten disciplines:** "Daley Thompson." *Encyclopedia Britannica*, s.v. "Daley Thompson," accessed July 8, 2024, https://www.britannica.com/biography/Daley-Thompson; "Daley Thompson," International Olympic Committee, https://olympics.com/en/athletes/daley-thompson; "Black History Month: The Story of Daley Thompson" *Team GB*, October 22, 2020, https://www.teamgb.com/article/black-history-month-the-story-of-daley-thompson/3HV3fvlSxFP4JNO5f5eWzQ.

44 **"It's not enough to win":** Rob Bagchi, "50 Stunning Olympic Moments No21: Daley Thompson Wins 1984 Decathlon," *The*

Guardian, April 4, 2012, https://www.theguardian.com/sport/
blog/2012/apr/04/50-stunning-olympic-moments-daley-
thompson.

45   **Tiny Buddha blog:** Stephen Guise, How Simple Mini Habits Can
Change Your Life," accessed July 8, 2024, Tiny Buddha, https://
tinybuddha.com/blog/simple-mini-habits-can-change-life/.

45   **superhabits:** Philosophers argue whether the Latin word *habitus*,
which Aquinas uses, is properly translated as "habit." In the last
century, Yves Simon and Anton Pegis had a long and apparently "less
and less polite" correspondence on the question. Yves Simon, *The
Definition of Moral Virtue* (New York: Fordham University Press,
1986), 57. Ezra Sullivan analyzes the debate and concludes that
"*habitus* bears a number of related analogous meanings and the
transliteration 'habit' accurately translates a number of meanings
contained in the term *habitus*. By using the word 'habit' to name
these interrelated realities, as Aquinas himself used the polyvalent
word *habitus*, we will be better positioned to understand how
mechanical habits are related to acquired virtuous habits and how
both are related to habits infused by God." Ezra Sullivan, *Habits
Holiness: Ethics, Theology, and Biopsychology* (Washington, D.C.: The
Catholic University of America Press, 2021), 34. Other
contemporary scholars agree, like Thomas Osborne, *Thomas
Aquinas on Virtue* (Cambridge: Cambridge University Press, 2022).
It seems safe to proceed with translating *habitus* as habit, particularly
for a book with a popular focus, such as this one.

45   **why haven't I heard more about them?:** Alasdair MacIntyre, *After
Virtue* (Notre Dame, IN: University of Notre Dame Press, 1984).
After Virtue inspired much of the contemporary recovery of interest
in virtue. The book provides a comprehensive account of how the
idea of virtue went from being nearly universally accepted to highly
controversial.

46   **better financial security:** T. E. Moffitt et al., "A Gradient of
Childhood Self-Control Predicts Health, Wealth, and Public Safety,"
Proceedings of the National Academy of Sciences 108, vol. 7 (2011):
2693–2698, https://doi.org/10.1073/pnas.1010076108.

46 **greater quality of life:** D. E. Davis et al., "Relational Humility: Conceptualizing and Measuring Humility as a Personality Judgment," *Journal of Personality Assessment* 93, no. 3 (2011): 225–234, https://doi.org/10.1080/00223891.2011.558871; E. J. Krumrei-Mancuso et al., "Links between Intellectual Humility and Acquiring Knowledge," *The Journal of Positive Psychology* 15, no. 2 (2019): 155–170, https://doi.org/10.1080/17439760.2019.1579359.

46 **lower anxiety, depression, and stress:** L. L. Toussaint, E. L. Worthington Jr., and D. R. Williams, eds., *Forgiveness and Health: Scientific Evidence and Theories Relating Forgiveness to Better Health* (New York: Springer, 2015), https://doi.org/10.1007/978-94-017-9993-5; L. Toussaint et al., "Effects of Lifetime Stress Exposure on Mental and Physical Health in Young Adulthood: How Stress Degrades and Forgiveness Protects Health," *Journal of Health Psychology* 21, no. 6 (2016): 1004–1014, https://doi.org/10.1177/1359105314544132.

46 **greater job performance, academic achievement, and well-being:** B. Aeon, A. Faber, and A. Panaccio, "Does Time Management Work? A Meta-analysis," *PLoS One* 16, no. 1 (2021): e0245066, doi.org/10.1371/journal.pone.0245066.

46 **overall greater well-being and happiness:** J. N. Hook et al., "Minimalism, Voluntary Simplicity, and Well-Being: A Systematic Review of the Empirical Literature," *The Journal of Positive Psychology* 18, no. 1 (October 2021): 1–12.

47 **experience all of the health, wellness, and life success benefits of each:** Some people might object that what we're doing here is "instrumentalizing" virtue. To be fully virtuous, an act must be done for its own sake. Is proposing the development of superhabits contrary to that? I think not. I agree with Nancy Snow's argument, summarized by Lamb, Brooks, and Brant, that "Developing virtues instrumental to a particular role (such as 'good employee') may, over time, lead an individual to shift from seeing virtue as primarily instrumental to recognizing the constitutive value of its contribution to flourishing and the intrinsic value of acting virtuously for its own sake." Michael Lamb, Edward Brooks, and Jonathan Brant, "Character Education in the University: Opportunities and

Challenges," in *Cultivating Virtue in the University*, ed. Michael Lamb, Edward Brooks, and Jonathan Brant (Oxford: Oxford University Press, 2022), 261; citing Nancy E. Snow, "From 'Ordinary' Virtue to Aristotelian Virtue," in *The Theory and Practice of Virtue Education*, ed. Tom Harrison and David I. Walker (London: Routledge, 2018), 67–81.

47 **But you already *have* all of them:** In philosophical terms, you have them in potential. Or at the risk of mixing metaphors, embryonically.

47 **You just have to activate them by exercising them:** I am grateful to Dr. Pat Fagan for first introducing me to the idea of virtues as muscles.

48 **generally helps us live better:** Adam Hadhazy, "How It's Possible for an Ordinary Person to Lift a Car" BBC, May 1, 2016, https://www.bbc.com/future/article/20160501-how-its-possible-for-an-ordinary-person-to-lift-a-car#; June Kloubec, "Pilates: How Does It Work and Who Needs It?." *Muscles, Ligaments and Tendons Journal* 1, no. 2 (April–June 2011): 61–66, https://www.ncbi.nlm.nih.gov/pmc/articles/PMC3666467/.

48 **not creating something new:** I have tried in this paragraph to show how "superhabit" goes beyond just a stable disposition to include the idea of *habitus* as a perfection of some capacity (Aquinas, *Summa Theologica* I-II, q. 49, art. 4).

48 **the same superhabits appear again and again:** See especially K. Dahlsgaard, C. Peterson, and M. E. P. Seligman, "Shared Virtue: The Convergence of Valued Human Strengths across Culture and History," *Review of General Psychology* 9, no. 3 (2005): 203–213, https://psycnet.apa.org/record/2018-70035-001. Philosopher Yves Simon calls the consensus on the cardinal virtues in particular "truly remarkable," one that "is not often found in the history of philosophy." Simon, *The Definition of Moral Virtue*, 95.

CHAPTER 5: "GENTLEFIRMNESS"

54 **A cage would have been helpful:** "NBA Players and Fans Brawl at Infamous 'Malice at the Palace' Game," History, A&E, November 16,

2021, https://www.history.com/this-day-in-history/sports-brawls-nba-infamous; Kristen Fleming, "Metta World Peace: 'I Wish I Had Trusted More People' with My Mental Health Struggle," *New York Post*, May 29, 2019, https://nypost.com/2019/05/29/metta-world-peace-i-wish-i-had-trusted-more-people-with-my-mental-health-struggle/; *Untold: Malice at the Palace*, Netflix, 2021, https://www.netflix.com/title/81026439; Andrew Lawrence, "Malice at the Palace: How a New Doc Re-examines the Epochal NBA Brawl," *Guardian*, August 10, 2021, https://www.theguardian.com/sport/2021/aug/10/untold-malice-at-the-palace-pistons-pacers-documentary; Robert W. Peterson, "When the Court Was a Cage," *Sports Illustrated*, November 11, 1991, https://vault.si.com/vault/1991/11/11/when-the-court-was-a-cage-in-the-early-days-of-pro-basketball-the-players-were-segregated-from-the-fans.

54   **Anger is the feeling we get:** More precisely, "when something gets in the way of a desired outcome or when we believe there's a violation of the way things should be." Brené Brown, *Atlas of the Heart* (New York: Random House, 2021), 220.

54   **that anger motivates action:** Ursula Hess, "Anger Is a Positive Emotion," in *The Positive Side of Negative Emotions*, ed. W. Gerrod Parrott (New York: Guilford Press, 2014), 57; L. F. Lowenstein, "Anger — Has It a Positive as Well as Negative Value? (Recent Research into Causes, Associated Features, Diagnosis and Treatment, 1998–2003)," *Journal of Human Behavior in the Social Environment* 9, no. 3 (2004): 21–40, https://psycnet.apa.org/record/2004-18857-002.

55   **An immediate cease-fire was ordered:** Trent Angers, *The Forgotten Hero of My Lai: The Hugh Thompson Story*, rev. ed. (Lafayette, LA: Acadian House, 2014).

55   **"This was not his idea of being an American soldier":** "Interview: Larry Colburn," American Experience, accessed July 9, 2024, https://www.pbs.org/wgbh/americanexperience/features/my-lai-interview-larry-colburn/.

56   **velvet glove over an iron fist:** Lee, "An (the) Iron Hand (Fist) in (the) Velvet Glove," Phrase Finder, December 1, 2004, https://www.phrases.org.uk/bulletin_board/37/messages/594.html.

56 **But that word has become confused with weakness:** See Greg Laurie, "Meekness, Not Weakness," *Christian Post,* September 22, 2010, https://www.christianpost.com/news/meekness-not-weakness.html.

56 ***mansuetude*:** *Merriam-Webster*, s.v. "mansuetude," accessed July 9, 2024, https://www.merriam-webster.com/dictionary/mansuetude.

56 **Gentlefirmness is *not* a habit of quenching or stifling your anger:** Pieper, *The Four Cardinal Virtues*, 195.

57 **Meadlo, sobbing now, complied:** Angers, *The Forgotten Hero of My Lai*, 73.

57 **depression, anxiety, and physical pain:** C. D. Spielberger, S.S. Krasner, and E.P. Solomon, "The Experience, Expression, and Control of Anger," in *Individual Differences, Stress, and Health Psychology* (New York: Springer, 1988), 89–108 Stewart, J.L. et al., "Anger Style, Psychopathology, and Regional Brain Activity," Emotion 8, no. 5 (2008): 701–713, https://doi.org/10.1037/a0013447.

57 **higher risk of heart disease:** Lowenstein, "Anger"; Y. Chida and A. Steptoe, "The Association of Anger and Hostility with Future Coronary Heart Disease: A Meta-analytic Review of Prospective Evidence," *Journal of the American College of Cardiology* 53, no. 11 (2009): 936–946, https://doi.org/10.1016/j.jacc.2008.11.044.

57–58 **breathing, relaxing imagery, meditation:** A. B. Fennell, E. M. Benau, and R. A. Atchley, "A Single Session of Meditation Reduces of Physiological Indices of Anger in Both Experienced and Novice Meditators," *Consciousness and Cognition* 40 (February 2016): 54–66, https://doi.org/10.1016/j.concog.2015.12.010; M. Saini, "A Meta-analysis of the Psychological Treatment of Anger: Developing Guidelines for Evidence-Based Practice," *The Journal of the American Academy of Psychiatry and the Law* 37, no. 4 (2009): 473–488, https://pubmed.ncbi.nlm.nih.gov/20018996/.

58 ***Why We Get Mad*:** Ryan Martin, *Why We Get Mad: How to Use Your Anger for Positive Change* (New York: Penguin Random House, 2021).

58 **screaming, or pounding a pillow:** B. J. Bushman, "Does Venting Anger Feed or Extinguish the Flame? Catharsis, Rumination, Distraction, Anger and Aggressive Responding," *Personality and Social Psychology Bulletin* 28, no. 6 (2002): 724–731, https://doi.org/10.1177/0146167202289002.

58 **it is not itself the change:** Brown, *Atlas of the Heart*, 220–226.

58 **"anger is telling you that there's a problem":** Ryan Martin, "How to Be Angry," *Psyche*, accessed July 10, 2024, https://psyche.co/guides/anger-is-a-potent-beneficial-force-if-used-in-the-right-way.

CHAPTER 6: FORGIVENESS

63 **Nhanh lost her father:** Angers, *The Forgotten Hero of My Lai*, 188–189.

63 **buried under his relatives' corpses:** Eric Fish, " 'Descent into Darkness': Looking Back at the My Lai Massacre," Asia Society, September 18, 2017, https://asiasociety.org/blog/asia/descent-darkness-looking-back-my-lai-massacre.

63 **"So we could forgive them":** Jon Wiener, "Op-Ed: A Forgotten Hero Stopped the My Lai Massacre 50 Years Ago Today," *Los Angeles Times*, March 16, 2018, https://www.latimes.com/opinion/op-ed/la-oe-wiener-my-lai-hugh-thompson-20180316-story.html.

64 **The survivors of My Lai said:** Fish, "Descent into Darkness"; "Forgiveness: Letting Go of Grudges and Bitterness," Mayo Clinic, accessed July 10, 2024, https://www.mayoclinic.org/healthy-lifestyle/adult-health/in-depth/forgiveness/art-20047692#:~:text=It%20can%20help%20free%20you,the%20one%20who%20hurt%20you.

64 **"you can find true freedom":** Matthew Dicks, *Someday Is Today: 22 Simple, Actionable Ways to Propel Your Creative Life* (Novato, CA: New World Library, 2022), 122.

64 **Ron Artest:** He now goes by the name Metta Sandiford-Artest.

64 **They have since become good friends:** Will Starjacki, "Metta Sandiford-Artest Became Friends with a Fan That Started the 'Malice at the Palace,' " Basketball Network, July 13, 2022, https://

www.basketballnetwork.net/off-the-court/metta-world-peace-became-friends-with-a-fan-who-attacked-him-in-the-famous-incident-malice-at-the-palace#:~:text=John%20Green%2C%20the%20cup%2Dthrower,he%20and%20Ron%20speak%20daily.

64　**Forgiveness is the habit of moderating your response:** I have translated Aquinas's *mansuetudo* and *clementia* as "Gentlefirmness" and "Forgiveness" respectively. I gave the rationale for the former in the preceding chapter. The latter is usually translated as "clemency," but I avoided that word because it is mostly used now very narrowly, in reference to the commutation of death sentences by state governors. Aquinas distinguishes between the two of them as follows: "*Clementia* moderates external punishment, while *mansuetudo* properly mitigates the passion of anger." See Aquinas, *Summa Theologica* II-II, q. 157, art. 1, in *The Summa Theologiae of St. Thomas Aquinas*, 2nd rev. ed., trans. Fathers of the English Dominican Province (online ed., New Advent/Kevin Knight, 2017), https://www.newadvent.org/summa/3157.htm.

64　**You can't go back and change what happened:** Forgiveness is distinct from Restraint in that Restraint moderates desires that arise from within us, and Forgiveness moderates desires that are provoked by what has happened externally.

64　**lower levels of anxiety, depression, and stress:** L. L. Toussaint, G. S. Shields, and G. M. Slavich, "Forgiveness, Stress, and Health: A 5-Week Dynamic Parallel Process Study," *Annals of Behavioral Medicine* 50, no. 5 (October 2016): 727–735, https://doi.org/10.1007/s12160-016-9796-6.

64　**improved cholesterol levels, sleep, and blood pressure:** Toussaint, Worthington, and Williams, *Forgiveness and Health*; L. Toussaint et al., "Effects of Lifetime Stress Exposure on Mental and Physical Health in Young Adulthood: How Stress Degrades and Forgiveness Protects Health," *Journal of Health Psychology* 21, no. 6 (2016): 1004–1014, https://doi.org/10.1177/1359105314544132.

64　**Forgiveness therapy is even being used to help treat cancer:** Lorie Johnson, "The Deadly Consequences of Unforgiveness," June 22, 2015, CBN, https://www2.cbn.com/news/news/deadly-consequences-unforgiveness.

65 **Fred Snodgrass died:** "Fred Snodgrass, 86, Dead Ball Player Muffed 1912 Fly," *New York Times*, April 6, 1974, https://www.nytimes. com/1974/04/06/archives/fred-snodgrass-86-dead-ball-player-muffed-1912-fly.html, cited in Donald DeMarco, *The Many Faces of Virtue* (Steubenville, OH: Emmaus Road, 2000), 206.

65 **that dropped fly ball is what people remember:** Gabriel Schechter, "Fred Snodgrass," SABR, accessed July 16, 2024, https://sabr.org/ bioproj/person/fred-snodgrass/.

65 **individuals can learn to be more forgiving:** T. W. Baskin and R. D. Enright, "Intervention Studies on Forgiveness: A Meta-analysis, *Journal of Counseling and Development*, 82, no. 1 (2004): 79–90.

65 **helped alleviate symptoms of post-traumatic stress disorder:** G. L. Reed and R. D. Enright, "The Effects of Forgiveness Therapy on Depression, Anxiety, and Posttraumatic Stress for Women after Spousal Emotional Abuse," *Journal of Consulting and Clinical Psychology* 74, no. 5 (2006): 920–929, https://doi. org/10.1037/0022-006X.74.5.920.

65 *Forgive for Good*: Fred Luskin, *Forgive for Good: A Proven Prescription for Health and Happiness* (New York: HarperOne, 2003); Everett Worthington, *The Path to Forgiveness: Six Practical Sections for Becoming a More Forgiving Person*, November 1, 2011, https://static1. squarespace.com/static/518a85e9e4b04323d507813b/t/533c6be2e 4b0cf4885e38a3a/1396468706314/the-path-to-forgiveness-six-practical-sections-for-becoming-a-more-forgiving-person.pdf.

65 **two-thirds of Americans felt like they need more Forgiveness:** "Resources on Forgiveness," Fetzer Institute, accessed July 10, 2024, https://fetzer.org/resources/resources-forgiveness.

65 **lower burnout:** Wenrui Cao, Reine C. van der Wal, and Toon W. Taris, "The Benefits of Forgiveness at Work: A Longitudinal Investigation of the Time-Lagged Relations between Forgiveness and Work Outcomes," *Frontiers in Psychology* 12 (2021), https://doi. org/10.3389/fpsyg.2021.710984.

66 **a pleasant seventy-five degrees:** Weather data from "Honolulu, HI Weather History," Weather Underground, accessed July 10, 2024, https://www.wunderground.com/history/daily/us/hi/honolulu/ PHNL/date/2001-2-9, and "February 9, 2001 Weather History in Honolulu," Weather Spark, accessed July 10, 2024, https://weatherspark.com/h/d/139/2001/2/9/Historical-Weather-on-Friday-February-9-2001-in-Honolulu-Hawaii-United-States# Figures-CloudCover.

66 **the ship was struck by a submarine:** The following account is drawn from the U.S. Navy Record of Proceedings record of John B. Nathman et al., "Court of Inquiry into the Circumstances Surrounding the Collision between USS Greenville (SSN 772) and Japanese M/V Ehime Maru That Occurred off the Coast of Oahu, Hawaii on 9 February 2001," https://web.archive.org/ web/20210601122420/https://www.jag.navy.mil/library/ investigations/GREENEVILLE_Combined_COI_Rpt.pdf.

67 **"an engaged and personable leader":** Nathman et al., "Court of Inquiry," 10–11.

67 **"series and combination of individual negligence(s)":** Nathman et al., "Court of Inquiry," 102.

67 **"failure of the ship's contact management team":** Nathman et al., Court of Inquiry," 103.

67 **"self-confident in his own abilities":** Nathman et al., "Court of Inquiry," 10.

67 **"genius with a thousand helpers":** Jim Collins, *Good to Great: Why Some Companies Make the Leap … and Others Don't* (New York: HarperCollins, 2001).

68 **"give his crew the opportunity to grow": "** Nathman et al., Court of Inquiry," ibid.

68 **When leaders have high opinions of their own abilities:** Such leaders would also benefit from growth in the superhabit of Humility.

68 **improves organizational performance:** Emilio Domínguez-Escrig et al., "Improving Performance through Leaders' Forgiveness: The Mediating Role of Radical Innovation," *Personnel Review* 51, no. 1 (2022): https://repositori.uji.es/xmlui/bitstream/handle/10234/192589/73685.pdf?sequence=1&isAllowed=y.

70 **"the more control I gave up, the more command I got":** D. Michael Abrashoff, *It's Your Ship* (New York: Grand Central, 2012): 32–33.

CHAPTER 7: ORDERLINESS

73 **state-wide recognition:** See " 'Ohana Health Plan Honors Case Managers for Dedication to Exceptional Care and Service," PR Newswire, December 21, 2016, https://www.prnewswire.com/news-releases/ohana-health-plan-honors-case-managers-for-dedication-to-exceptional-care-and-service-300382355.html; " 'Ohana Health Plan Honored Case Managers for Dedication to Providing Outstanding Services," PR Newswire, November 6, 2017, https://www.prnewswire.com/news-releases/ohana-health-plan-honored-case-managers-for-dedication-to-providing-outstanding-services-300549637.html.

73 **(GTD) system:** David Allen, *Getting Things Done: The Art of Stress-Free Productivity* (New York: Penguin Books, 2003).

74 **And he sleeps better:** "Aliman's GTD Story," GTD, October 22, 2018, https://gettingthingsdone.com/2018/10/alimans-gtd-story/.

74 **(MBTI):** See "the Preferences: E-I, S-N, T-F, J-P," Myers & Briggs Foundation, accessed July 10, 2024, https://www.myersbriggs.org/my-mbti-personality-type/the-mbti-preferences/; "The Four Preferences," PersonalityPage, accessed July 10, 2024, https://personalitypage.com/html/four-prefs.html.

74 **Ryder Carroll struggled:** Ryder Carroll, *The Bullet Journal Method* (New York: Penguin Random House, 2018).

75 **"Through trial and *a lot* of error":** Ibid., 4 (italics in original).

75 **It is the superhabit for getting work done by figuring out in what sequence to do things:** Aquinas, citing Andronicus of Rhodes, calls it "method," which enables you to "discern what to do and what not to do, and to observe the right order, and to persevere in what we do." Aquinas, *Summa Theologica* II-II, q. 168, art. 1. That's all he says about "method," so discussion of this superhabit is largely drawn from the current empirical research.

75 **it still had a positive effect on well-being:** B. Aeon, A. Faber, and A. Panaccio, "Does Time Management Work? A Meta-analysis," *PLoS One*, 16, no. 1 (2021): e0245066, doi.org/10.1371/journal.pone.0245066.

76 **your brain doesn't have to work as hard to find things:** Stephanie McMains and Sabine Kastner, "Interactions of Top-Down and Bottom-Up Mechanisms in Human Visual Cortex," *Journal of Neuroscience* 31, no. 2 (2011): 587–597, doi.org/10.1523/jneurosci.3766-10.2011.

76 **Disorganized environments ... cause stress:** See, for example, D. E. Saxbe and R. Repetti, "No Place like Home: Home Tours Correlate with Daily Patterns of Mood and Cortisol," *Personality and Social Psychology Bulletin* 36, no. 1 (2010): 71–81, https://doi.org/10.1177/0146167209352864.

76 **marital stability, and well-being:** M. P. Wilmot, and D. S. Ones, "A Century of Research on Conscientiousness at Work," *Proceedings of the National Academy of Sciences* 116, no. 46 (2019): 23004–23010, https://doi.org/10.1073/pnas.1908430116.

76 **higher quality of life in both children and adults:** Saxbe and Repetti, "No Place like Home."

77 **Tynan:** "About me (Tynan)," Tynan.com, accessed July 10, 2024, https://tynan.com/about/.

77 **"His home secures, vacuums, heats, and cools itself":** Joseph Reagle, *Hacking Life: Systematized Living and Its Discontents* (Boston: MIT Press, 2019), 26.

77 **Reale argues that life hackers:** Ibid., 12.

77   **Tynan's book:** Tynan, *Superhuman by Habit: A Guide to Becoming the Best Possible Version of Yourself, One Tiny Habit at a Time* (Scotts Valley, CA: CreateSpace, 2014).

77   **"appointment books in which every moment has been sold in advance":** Hans Urs von Balthasar, *Unless You Become like This Child*, trans. Erasmo Leiva-Merikakis (San Francisco: Ignatius Press, 1991), 54.

78   **Since there are significant costs to switching:** J. S. Rubinstein, D. E. Meyer, and J. E. Evans, "Executive Control of Cognitive Processes in Task Switching," *Journal of Experimental Psychology: Human Perception and Performance* 27, no. 4 (2001): 763–797, https://doi.org/10.1037/0096-1523.27.4.763; E. Ophir, C. Nass, and A. D. Wagner, "Cognitive Control in Media Multitaskers," *Proceedings of the National Academy of Sciences* 106, no. 37 (2009): 15583–15587, doi.org/10.1073/pnas.0903620106. "Attention residue" is part of the switching cost. Sophie Leroy, "Why Is It so Hard to Do My Work? The Challenge of Attention Residue When Switching between Work Tasks," *Organizational Behavior and Human Decision Processes* 109, no. 2 (July 2009): 168–181, https://www.sciencedirect.com/science/article/abs/pii/S0749597809000399?via%3Dihub.

78   **they also cause stress:** Harshad Puranik, Joel Koopman, and Heather C. Vough, "Pardon the Interruption: An Integrative Review and Future Research Agenda for Research on Work Interruptions," *Journal of Management* 46, no. 6 (2020): 806–842, https://doi.org/10.1177/0149206319887428.

78   **These things have all been demonstrated to improve organizational skills:** D. J. Britton-Rumohr and A. L. Lannie, "Adapting an Evidence Based Tier 3 Organizational Skill Intervention to Improve Classwide Organizational Skills," *Journal of Applied School Psychology* 38, no. 2 (2022): 1–25, https://doi.org/10.1080/15377903.2021.1911898.

78   **"You don't go to the grocery store with a list of what you don't want":** Liz Guber, "Molly Owens Is the Force behind Our Collective Obsession with Personality Tests," Girlboss, accessed July 10, 2024, https://girlboss.com/blogs/read/enneagram-personality-test-truity.

79 **"pomodoro technique":** The Pomodoro Technique, accessed July 10, 2024, https://www.pomodorotechnique.com/book-pomodoro-technique.php.

79 **sharing aspirations with a friend or colleague:** Molly Owens, "6 Tips to Help Perceivers Overcome the Productivity Slump," *True You*, Truity, August 17, 2016, https://www.truity.com/blog/6-tips-help-perceivers-overcome-productivity-slump.

79 **"Golden Hour":** OptimalWork, accessed July 10, 2024, https://optimalwork.com.

79 **the following ideas that author Kevin Kruse gathered:** Kevin Kruse, *15 Secrets Successful People Know about Time Management: The Productivity Habits of 7 Billionaires, 13 Olympic Athletes, 29 Straight-A Students, and 239 Entrepreneurs* (Toronto: Kruse Group, 2015); Kevin Kruse, "15 Secrets of Ultra-productive People," Medium, February 22, 2016, https://medium.com/@kruse/15-secrets-of-ultra-productive-people-4e38a86ca011.

CHAPTER 8: EUTRAPELIA

85 **Theodore Edward Hook:** My source for the following is the biography of Thomas Hook, written by the Rev. Dalton Barnham, *The Life and Remains of Theodore Edward Hook* (London: Bentley, 1849).

85 **"I beg your pardon, sir":** Ibid, 54–55. I have modified the dialog very slightly to prevent the older English getting in the way of comprehension.

87 **"Berners Street Hoax":** Ibid., 73.

87 **Mrs. Tottenham:** Sarah Murden, based on her own research, concludes that the victim's real name was Tottingham, not Tottenham. Sarah Murden, "Berners Street Hoax — True or False?," *All Things Georgian*, July 4, 2022, https://georgianera.wordpress.com/2022/07/04/berners-street-hoax-true-or-false/. For consistency's sake, I have decided to use the name given by Barham, my original source.

88 **"the poor old lady":** Barnham, *Life and Remains*, 74.

90 **The vice of "frivolity":** *Oxford Learners Dictionary* defines "frivolity" as "behavior that is silly or funny, especially when this is not suitable," which seems apt.

90 **The third type of excessive playfulness:** Aquinas, *Summa Theologica* II-II, q. 168, art. 2.

90 ***mirthlessness:*** Aquinas, *Summa Theologica* II-II, q. 168, art. 3 notes that lack of mirth is the vice that opposes Eutrapelia through a deficiency of playfulness.

90 **Studies show that playful adults have greater life satisfaction:** René T. Proyer, "The Well-Being of Playful Adults," *European Journal of Humour Research* 1, no. 1 (2013): 84–98, https://europeanjournalofhumour.org/index.php/ejhr/article/view/Rene%20Proyer/Rene%20Proyer.

90 **my way of avoiding thinking about significant areas of my life:** Pieper, in *A Brief Reader on the Virtues of the Human Heart*, trans. Paul C. Duggan (San Francisco: Ignatius Press, 1991), 51–52, argues that a resistance to authentic leisure is a form of sloth (*acedia*) in that it's a form of refusing to assent to the fullness of your calling as a human being.

91 **John Garvey … gives a couple of good analogies:** Garvey, *The Virtues*, 180.

91 **"quiet desperation":** H. D. Thoreau, *Walden* (New York: Crowell, 1910), 8.

93 **Even while you sleep, your brain continues to be active:** "What Happens in the Brain during Sleep?," *Scientific American*, September 1, 2015, https://www.scientificamerican.com/article/what-happens-in-the-brain-during-sleep1/.

93 **According to ancient and medieval philosophers:** Aquinas, *Summa Theologica* II-II, q. 168, art. 2, citing I-II, q. 25, art. 2. "Now it is evident that whatever tends to an end, has, in the first place, an aptitude or proportion to that end, for nothing tends to a disproportionate end; secondly, it is moved to that end; thirdly, it rests in the end, after having attained it. And this very aptitude or

proportion of the appetite to good is love, which is complacency in good; while movement towards good is desire or concupiscence; and rest in good is joy or pleasure." At Logic Museum, http://www. logicmuseum.com/wiki/Authors/Thomas_Aquinas/Summa_ Theologiae/Part_IIa/Q25#q25a2arg1.

93 **playing games can improve cognitive function:** Nicola Ferreira et al., "Associations between Cognitively Stimulating Leisure Activities, Cognitive Function and Age-Related Cognitive Decline," *International Journal of Geriatric Psychiatry* 30, no. 4 (April 2015): 422–430, https://onlinelibrary.wiley.com/doi/abs/10.1002/ gps.4155.

93 **having hobbies can lower dementia risk:** P. Almeida-Meza, A. Steptoe, and D. Cadar, "Is Engagement in Intellectual and Social Leisure Activities Protective Against Dementia Risk? Evidence from the English Longitudinal Study of Ageing," *Journal of Alzheimer's Disease* 80, no. 2 (2021): 555–565, https://content.iospress.com/ articles/journal-of-alzheimers-disease/jad200952.

93 **leisure activities improve both mental and physical health:** Linda L. Caldwell, "Leisure and Health: Why Is Leisure Therapeutic?," *British Journal of Guidance & Counselling* 33, no. 1 (2005): 7–26, doi. org/10.1080/03069880412331335939; Daisy Fancourt et al., "How Leisure Activities Affect Health: A Narrative Review and Multi-level Theoretical Framework of Mechanisms of Action," *Lancet* 8, no. 4 (April 2021): 329–339, https://doi.org/10.1016/S2215-0366 (20)30384-9.

93 **"enjoyment is rest for the soul":** "Quies autem animae est delectatio." Aquinas, *Summa Theologica* II-II, q. 168, art. 2. *Delectatio* is usually translated as "pleasure," but Deferrari gives "amusement, delight, enjoyment," and I think "enjoyment" is best here.

94 **If you're trying to achieve something, then your mind is at work:** John Dattilo and Francisco Javier Lopez Frias, "A Critical Examination of Leisure in Modernity: Rejecting Instrumentalism and Embracing Flourishing," *Journal of Leisure Research* 52, no. 5 (2021): 581–598, doi.org/10.1080/00222216.2020.1789013.

95   **Staples advertising campaign:** Jane L. Levere, "Press a Button and Your Worries Are Gone," *New York Times,* July 21, 2008, https://www.nytimes.com/2008/07/21/business/media/21Adnewsletter1.html.

96   **none of them are leisure:** See Walter Kerr's *The Decline of Pleasure* (New York: Simon and Schuster, 1962). This is a fascinating, book-length treatment of false approaches to leisure, and a worthwhile read.

96   **Research by the National Center on Addiction and Substance Abuse at Columbia University:** *The Importance of Family Dinners VIII* (New York: The National Center on Addiction and Substance Abuse at Columbia University, 2012), https://www.fmi.org/docs/default-source/familymeals/2012924familydinnersviii.pdf?sfvrsn=967c676e_2.

CHAPTER 9: THE SUPERHABITS SYSTEM

99   **Scientists have mapped the human genome:** Laura M. Zahn, "Filling the Gaps," *Science* 376, no. 6588 (2022): 42–43, https://www.science.org/doi/10.1126/science.abp8653.

99   **Unfortunately, they can't seem to agree on how many there are:** For a comprehensive account of how we came to have this dueling lists of virtues, see Alasdair MacIntyre's *After Virtue.*

99   **Epictetus had four:** Epictetus, *The Discourses of Epictetus: With the Encheiridion and Fragments,* trans. and ed. George Long (London: Bell, 1916). William J. Bennett, ed., *The Book of Virtues: A Treasury of Great Moral Stories* (New York: Simon and Schuster, 1993); Benjamin Franklin, *The Autobiography of Benjamin Franklin* (New York: Simon and Schuster, 2004); Romano Guardini, *The Virtues: On Forms of Moral Life,* trans. Stella Lange (Chicago: Regnery, 1967); C. Peterson and M. E. P. Seligman, *Character Strengths and Virtues: A Handbook and Classification* (Oxford: Oxford University Press, 2004); Garvey, *The Virtues.*

101   **"MECE":** For a detailed description of the MECE approach to problem-solving, see Ethan M. Rasiel and Paul N. Friga, *The*

McKinsey Mind: Understanding and Implementing the Problem-Solving Tools and Management Techniques of the World's Top Strategic Consulting Firm (New York: McGraw-Hill, 2001).

101 **he had developed a "MECE" analysis of all of human life:** Peterson and Seligman's classification of positive psychology's twenty-four character strengths includes "mutually exclusive and exhaustive subcategories." But in that system, it's not the virtues or character strengths (superhabits) that are mutually exclusive or exhaustive, it's the *categories*. As to the character strengths themselves, it remains "open to the possibility of consolidating those that prove empirically indistinguishable, as well as adding new strengths that are distinct." Peterson and Seligman, *Character Strengths and Virtues*, 6 and 8. While this classification has proven to be helpful, it wasn't intended to provide *completeness*. It will tell you which bucket to put each superhabit in, but it won't tell you if any given bucket is full, if you've gathered all the relevant superhabits for that bucket.

102 **He then divided our practical lives:** It's important to note that when I use the word *divide*, or other similar words (so as not to keep repeating the word *distinguish*), I don't mean actually separating from each other — I just mean distinguish conceptually, for the sake of understanding better. I am never for a moment suggesting that, say, one part of your day should be dedicated to dealing with feelings, and another to dealing with action. Clearly, I hope, many of these things happen simultaneously in any given day.

102 **eighty-seven different emotions:** Brown, *Atlas of the Heart*.

103 **each of these cardinal superhabits had several other superhabits associated with it:** In *Summa Theologica* II-II, q. 143, Aquinas distinguishes among three types of "parts." He explains that these parts are of three kinds: integral, subjective, and potential. For the purposes of this book, these distinctions do not seem to be necessary, and so I have avoided referring to them.

104 **Courage, Practical Wisdom, and Justice:** The superhabits for our intellectual and spiritual lives are included, for completeness' sake, in appendix A.

CHAPTER 10: SELF-DISCIPLINE

110 **One will not survive:** Jim Slauson, aged seventy-five, was making his second attempt at the Everglades Challenge, when he disappeared off the southwest coast of Florida. His boat was found, but his body was never recovered. It is assumed that he fell overboard and drowned, likely as a result of a heart attack or stroke. Tony Marrero, "A St. Pete Sailor Dreamed of an Epic Adventure. Then, He Disappeared," *Tampa Bay Times*, May 29, 2020, https://www.tampabay.com/news/pinellas/2020/05/27/a-st-pete-sailor-dreamed-of-an-epic-adventure-then-he-disappeared/.

110 **"the real world":** WaterTribe, Facebook, https://www.facebook.com/groups/440773022707818/permalink/7114247338693653/, and personal communication.

110 *misogi:* "Find Your Misogi," *Valet*, accessed July 11, 2024, https://www.valetmag.com/the-handbook/living/misogi-challenge.php.

110 **"battle to overcome the physical and mental demons":** WaterTribe, Facebook.

111 **Self-Discipline, or Self-control:** The Latin name for Self-Discipline is *temperantia*, which is usually translated as "Temperance." But that word, like so many of the other traditional words, has been severely narrowed in its meaning. Temperance now mostly connotes not drinking alcohol to excess. But as we'll see below, there's a separate superhabit for that, Sobriety, which is just one of the many superhabits that make up Courage.

111 **"career accomplishments":** Martin E. P. Seligman and Ed Royzman, "Authentic Happiness," University of Pennsylvania, July 2003, https://www.authentichappiness.sas.upenn.edu/newsletters/authentichappiness/happiness#:~:text=Desire%20theory%20holds%20that%20that,did%20not%20much%20desire%20pleasure.

112 **ignoring or repressing our desires:** See ibid. We are not referring here, of course, to desires for harmful things.

112 **cultivated, channeled:** This is the work of the cardinal virtue of Self-Discipline. Aquinas, *Summa Theologica* II-II, q. 141, art. 1.

"Aquinas maintains that the passions naturally obey reason and that over time reason's guidance becomes embedded in the sense appetite." Nicholas E. Lombardo, "Passion, Reason, and Virtue," in *The Logic of Desire: Aquinas on Emotion* (Washington D.C.: The Catholic University of America Press, 2011), 94. https://doi.org/10.2307/j.ctt3fgpxp.8.

112 **Recent research supports Aquinas's view:** See, e.g., Nicole L. Mead and Vanessa M. Patrick, "The Taming of Desire: Unspecific postponement Reduces Desire for and Consumption of Postponed Temptations," *Journal of Personality and Social Psychology* 110, no. 1 (January 2016): 20–35.

113 **feelings against (fears) and feelings for (desires):** Aquinas, *Summa Theologica* I-II, q. 61, art. 2 and elsewhere refers to them as "irascible" and "concupiscible" passions. These are not precisely the same as fears and desires, but they are close enough for the purposes of this book.

113 **what we want right now, and how we want to live:** I am following here Aquinas's division of Self-Discipline into its subjective and potential parts, *Summa Theologica* II-II, q. 143.

114 **There are two superhabits for how we move:** St. Thomas distinguished between two types of *modestia*, usually translated as "Modesty": (1) relating to outward appearances, which I have translated as "Modesty," and (2) relating to outward movements of the body. This latter is further subdivided into two other virtues: "Hence Andronicus [*De Affectibus*] ascribes two things to these outward movements: namely 'taste' [*ornatum*] which regards what is becoming to the person, wherefore he says that it is the knowledge of what is becoming in movement and behavior; and 'methodicalness' [*bona ordinatio*] which regards what is becoming to the business in hand, and to one's surroundings, wherefore he calls it 'the practical knowledge of separation,' i.e. of the distinction of 'acts.'" Aquinas, *Summa Theologica* II-II, q. 168, art. 1, in *The Summa Theologiae of St. Thomas Aquinas*, https://www.newadvent.org/summa/3168.htm. Instead of "taste" I use the word "Gravitas," and instead of "methodicalness," I use "Orderliness" (chap. 7). In Aquinas, *Summa Theologica* II-II, q. 143, for what is becoming in movement, he

mentions not just *ornatus*/Gravitas, but also *austeritas*, which I'm calling "Litheness."

115 **"Stand up straight with your shoulders back":** Peterson, *12 Rules for Life*, 28.

115 **open "power" posture leads to greater confidence:** D. R. Carney, A. J. C. Cuddy, and A. J. Yap, "Power Posing: Brief Nonverbal Displays Affect Neuroendocrine Levels and Risk Tolerance," *Psychological Science* 21, no. 10 (2010): 1363–1368, doi. org/10.1177/0956797610383437. Subsequent research has reaffirmed the first part of her findings (about confidence), though some argue that there is still insufficient evidence for the second part (about testosterone); A. J. C. Cuddy, S. J. Schultz, and N. E. Fosse, "*P*-curving a More Comprehensive Body of Research on Postural Feedback Reveals Clear Evidential Value for Power-Posing Effects: Reply to Simmons and Simonsohn (2017)," *Psychological Science* 29, no. 4 (2018): 656–666, https://doi.org/10.1177/ 0956797617746749. For a good summary of the debate, see Kim Elsesser, "Power Posing Is Back: Amy Cuddy Successfully Refutes Criticism," *Forbes*, April 3, 2018, https://www.forbes.com/sites/ kimelsesser/2018/04/03/power-posing-is-back-amy-cuddy-successfully-refutes-criticism/?sh=734cebe33b8e.

115 **"It is not daily increase but daily decrease":** "#52: Hack Away the Unessentials," Bruce Lee Enterprises, accessed July 11, 2024, https://brucelee.com/ podcast-blog/2017/6/28/52-hack-away-the-unessentials.

116 **sitting for extended periods of the day is more dangerous than smoking:** J. A. Levine, "Sick of Sitting," *Diabetologia* 58, no. 8 (2015): 1751–1758, doi.org/10.1007/s00125-015-3624-6; Ryan Fiorenzi, "Sitting Is the New Smoking," July 12, 2023, Start Standing, https://www.startstanding.org/sitting-new-smoking/.

116 **Dr. Kelly Starrett's encyclopedic book:** Kelly Starrett and Glen Cordoza, *Becoming a Supple Leopard: The Ultimate Guide to Resolving Pain, Preventing Injury, and Optimizing Athletic Performance* (Auberry, CA: Victory Belt, 2015).

116 **what you wear has a significant effect on what others think:** Leslie A. Zebrowitz and Joann M. Montepare, "Social Psychological Face Perception: Why Appearance Matters," *Social and Personality Psychology Compass* 2, no. 3 (2008): 1497, https://www.ncbi.nlm. nih.gov/pmc/articles/PMC2811283/; DongWon Oh, Eldar Shafir, and Alexander Todorov, "Economic Status Cues from Clothes Affect Perceived Competence from Faces," *Nature Human Behaviour* 4, no. 3 (2020): 287–293, https://pubmed.ncbi.nlm.nih.gov/31819209/.

116 **Our physical desires:** In Aquinas, *Summa Theologica* II-II, q. 143, Aquinas includes only the virtues of nourishment and sex as subjective parts of Temperance (what I have described as "physical desires"), because they are the pleasures of touch, and thus proper to Temperance. All the rest, including those related to external goods, he considers potential parts (I'm calling them "mental desires"). I believe that in our society, the desire for "stuff" is so strong, that it's worth considering among the subjective parts, which is why I've moved it here. See, e.g., M. A. Bauer et al., "Cuing Consumerism: Situational Materialism Undermines Personal and Social Well-Being," *Psychological Science* 23, no. 5 (2012): 517–523, https://doi. org/10.1177/0956797611429579; T. Kasser, *The High Price of Materialism* (Cambridge, MA: MIT Press, 2003).

117 **less likely to develop clinical eating disorders:** C. C. Horwath, D. Hagmann, and C. Hartmann, "The Power of Food: Self-Control Moderates the Association of Hedonic Hunger with Overeating, Snacking Frequency and Palatable Food Intake," *Eating Behaviors* 38 (August 2020): 101393, https://doi.org/10.1016/j.eatbeh.2020. 101393; C. Georgii et al., "The Dynamics of Self-Control: Within-Participant Modeling of Binary Food Choices and Underlying Decision Processes as a Function of Restrained Eating," *Psychological Research* 84, no. 7 (2020): 1777–1788, https://doi.org/10.1007/ s00426-019-01185-3; Will Crescioni et al., "High Trait Self-Control Predicts Positive Health Behaviors and Success in Weight Loss," *Journal of Health Psychology* 16, no. 5 (2011): 750–759, https://doi. org/10.1177/1359105310390247; C. Davis et al., "Immediate Pleasures and Future Consequences: A Neuropsychological Study of Binge Eating and Obesity," *Appetite* 54, no. 1 (February 2010): 208–213, https://doi.org/10.1016/j.appet.2009.11.002.

117 **Abstemiousness can be enhanced by practices like making a daily food log:** J. Daubenmier et al., "Effects of a Mindfulness-Based Weight Loss Intervention in Adults with Obesity: A Randomized Clinical Trial," *Obesity* 24, no. 4 (April 2016): 794–804, https://doi.org/10.1002/oby.21396; G. A. O'Reilly et al., "Mindfulness-Based Interventions for Obesity-Related Eating Behaviours: A Literature Review," *Obesity Reviews* 15, no. 6 (June 2014): 453–461, https://doi.org/10.1111/obr.12156. One study showed that following pre-eating rituals consistently can enhance subjective feelings of Self-Discipline and assist in increasing self-control, but that study has since been retracted due to errors. A. D. Tian et al., "Enacting Rituals to Improve Self-Control," *Journal of Personality and Social Psychology* 114, no. 6 (2018): 851–876, https://doi.org/10.1037/pspa0000113.

117 *Hara hachi bu***:** "Don't Eat until You're Full — Instead, Mind Your Hara Hachi Bu Point," Cleveland Clinic, May 10, 2019, https://health.clevelandclinic.org/dont-eat-until-youre-full-instead-mind-your-hara-hachi-bu-point.

118 **Sobriety . . . is associated with physical health benefits:** X. I. Yao et al., "Change in Moderate Alcohol Consumption and Quality of Life: Evidence from 2 Population-Based Cohorts," *Canadian Medical Association Journal* 191, no. 27 (2019): E753–E760, https://doi.org/10.1503/cmaj.181583.

118 **consuming alcohol in moderate amounts reduces stress:** C. Baum-Baicker, "The Psychological Benefits of Moderate Alcohol Consumption: A Review of the Literature," *Drug and Alcohol Dependence* 15, no. 4 (August 1985): 305–322, https://doi.org/10.1016/0376-8716(85)90008-0; K. Mezue et al., "Alcohol's Beneficial Effect on Cardiovascular Disease Is Partially Mediated through Modulation of Stress-Associated Brain Activity," *Journal of the American College of Cardiology* 77, no. 18 (2021): 6, https://doi.org/10.1016/s0735-1097(21)01349-8.

118 **At the risk of stating the obvious:** G. A. Colditz, S. E. Philpott, and S. E. Hankinson, "The Impact of the Nurses' Health Study on Population Health: Prevention, Translation, and Control," *American Journal of Public Health* 106, no. 9 (September 2016): 1540–1545, https://doi.org/10.2105/AJPH.2016.303343.

118 Excessive alcohol consumption: M. Grønbaek, "The Positive and
Negative Health Effects of Alcohol — and the Public Health
Implications," *Journal of Internal Medicine* 265, no. 4 (April 2009):
407–420, https://doi.org/10.1111/j.1365-2796.2009.02082.x.

118 memory problems, and mental health problems: J. Rehm et al.,
"The Relation between Different Dimensions of Alcohol
Consumption and Burden of Disease: An Overview, *Addiction* 105,
no. 5 (May 2010): 817–843, https://doi.org/10.1111/j.1360-
0443.2010.02899.x.

118 Drinking habits can be improved by tracking consumption: R. K.
Hester, H. D. Delaney, and W. Campbell, "ModerateDrinking.Com
and Moderation Management: Outcomes of a Randomized Clinical
Trial with Non-dependent Problem Drinkers," *Journal of Consulting
and Clinical Psychology* 79, no. 2 (2011): 215–224, https://doi.
org/10.1037/a0022487.

119 Some people will consume alcohol because of peer pressure: H.
Morris et al., "Peer Pressure and Alcohol Consumption in Adults
Living in the UK: A Systematic Qualitative Review," *BMC Public
Health* 20, no. 1014 (2020), https://doi.org/10.1186/
s12889-020-09060-2.

119 she would order a gin and tonic: Fiorina, *Tough Choices*, 31.

119 Aquinas quotes this famous line: Aquinas, *Summa Theologica* II-II,
q. 147, art. 1, Aquinas attributes it to Jerome, who was quoting
Terence.

119 Interestingly, while fasting reduces testosterone: Raidh A. Talib
et al., "The Effect of Fasting on Erectile Function and Sexual Desire
on Men in the Month of Ramadan," *Urology Journal* 12, no. 2
(2015): 2099–2102, https://pubmed.ncbi.nlm.nih.gov/25923156/;
Sofia Cienfuegos et al., "Effect of Intermittent Fasting on
Reproductive Hormone Levels in Females and Males: A Review of
Human Trials," *Nutrients* 14, no. 11 (2022): 2343, doi.org/10.3390/
nu14112343.

119 **lower anxiety, depression, and distress:** D. Mollaioli et al., "Benefits of Sexual Activity on Psychological, Relational, and Sexual Health during the COVID-19 Breakout," *The Journal of Sexual Medicine* 18, no. 1 (January 2021): 35–49, https://doi. org/10.1016/j.jsxm.2020.10.008.

119 **healthy sexual behaviors are correlated with improved physical health:** H. Liu et al., "Is Sex Good for Your Health? A National Study on Partnered Sexuality and Cardiovascular Risk among Older Men and Women," *Journal of Health and Social Behavior* 57, no. 3 (2016): 276–296, https://doi.org/10.1177/0022146516661597; T. K. Lorenz, J. R. Heiman, and G. E. Demas, "Interactions among Sexual Activity, Menstrual Cycle Phase, and Immune Function in Healthy Women," *Journal of Sex Research* 55, no. 9 (2018): 1087–1095, https://doi.org/10.1080/00224499.2017.1394961.

119 **Extensive and much replicated research:** Nicholas H. Wolfinger, "Counterintuitive Trends in the Link between Premarital Sex and Marital Stability," IFS, June 6, 2016, https://ifstudies.org/blog/ counterintuitive-trends-in-the-link-between-premarital-sex-and-marital-stability.

120 **increases the chance of divorce:** Jesse Smith, "Testing Common Theories on the Relationship between Premarital Sex and Marital Stability," IFS, March 6, 2023, https://ifstudies.org/blog/ testing-common-theories-on-the-relationship-between-premarital-sex-and-marital-stability.

120 **feminist Louise Perry's book:** Louise Perry, *The Case against the Sexual Revolution* (Cambridge: Polity Press, 2022); Jason Evert, *If You Really Loved Me: 100 Questions on Dating, Relationships, and Sexual Purity* (Scottsdale, AZ: Totus Tuus Press, 2013).

120 **Research shows that it is associated with being less impulsive:** J. Lastovicka et al., "Lifestyle of the Tight and Frugal: Theory and Measurement," *Journal of Consumer Research* 26, no. 1 (June 1999): 85–98, https://doi.org/10.1086/209552; T. Kasser, "Frugality, Generosity, and Materialism in Children and Adolescents," in *What Do Children Need to Flourish?*, ed. K. A. Moore and L. H. Lippman

(New York: Springer, 2005), 357–373, https://doi.
org/10.1007/0-387-23823-9_22.

120 **The superhabit of Thrift … is commonly evident among
    successful entrepreneurs:** Sam Walton, *Made in America* (New
    York: Random House, 2012); Collins, *Good to Great*; David Green,
    More than a Hobby (Nashville, TN: Thomas Nelson, 2005); S. Truett
    Cathy, *Eat Mor Chikin: Inspire More People* (Decatur, GA: Looking
    Glass Books, 2002); Robert Luddy, *Entrepreneurial Life: The Path
    from Startup to Market Leader* (CaptiveAire, 2018); Quentin
    Skrebac, H. J. *Heinz: A Biography* (Jefferson, NC: McFarland, 2009);
    Mackenzie Busch, *The Paperboy* (Outskirts Press, 2020).

121 **lower well-being and mental health, and more behavioral
    disorders:** T. Kasser and R. M. Ryan, "A Dark Side of the American
    Dream: Correlates of Financial Success as a Central Life Aspiration,"
    Journal of Personality and Social Psychology 65, no. 2 (1993): 410–
    422, https://psycnet.apa.org/record/1993-45246-001.

121 **Corley found that millionaires tended to be surprisingly thrifty:**
    Tom Corley, "10 Common Millionaire Habits," Acorns Grow
    Incorporated, August 25, 2022, https://www.acorns.com/learn/
    earning/common-millionaire-habits/.

121 **YNAB published my story on their website:** Rachel Wong, "How I
    Got a Handle on My Finances," YNAB, February 5, 2021, https://
    www.ynab.com/blog/i-manage-a-multi-million-dollar-budget-
    at-work.

121 **avoiding wanting a lifestyle that is too luxurious:** For an in-depth
    philosophical and theological exploration of luxury as a vice, see
    David Cloutier, *The Vice of Luxury: Economic Excess in a Consumer
    Age* (Washington, D.C.: Georgetown University Press, 2015).

121 **An extensive review of twenty-three empirical studies:** J. N. Hook
    et al., "Minimalism, Voluntary Simplicity, and Well-Being: A
    Systematic Review of the Empirical Literature," *Journal of Positive
    Psychology* 18, no. 1 (October 2021): 1–12, https://doi.org/10.1080
    /17439760.2021.1991450.

122 **Other studies show lower stress:** L. Boujbel and A. D'Astous, "Voluntary Simplicity and Life Satisfaction: Exploring the Mediating Role of Consumption Desires," *Journal of Consumer Behaviour* 11, no. 6 (November/December 2012): 487–494, https://doi.org/10.1002/cb.1399.

122 **Research also shows a link with physical health:** H. Dittmar et al., "The Relationship between Materialism and Personal Well-Being: A Meta-analysis," *Journal of Personality and Social Psychology* 107, no. 5 (2014): 879–924, https://doi.org/10.1037/a0037409.

122 **"half-amused, half-disgusted":** Trennert, *My Side of the Street*, 51–52.

122 **Marie Kondo's celebrated book:** Marie Kondo, *The Life Changing Magic of Tidying Up: The Japanese Art of Decluttering and Organizing* (Emeryville, CA: Ten Speed Press, 2014). Not everyone likes this book. See, e.g., L. Ouellette, "Spark Joy? Compulsory Happiness and the Feminist Politics of Decluttering," *Culture Unbound* 11, nos. 3–4 (2019): 534–550, doi.org/10.3384/cu.2000.1525.191108.

CHAPTER 11: COURAGE

127 **"Never give in":** Winston Churchill, "Never Give In, Never, Never, Never, 1941," America's National Churchhill Museum, accessed July 12, 2024, https://www.nationalchurchillmuseum.org/never-give-in-never-never-never.html

127 **Churchill launched a convoy:** I originally delivered this account of the "Malta Convoy" and the USS *Ohio* as the 2022 graduation speech for The Heights School, Potomac, MD. My main sources for the following are Michael Pearson, *The Ohio and Malta: The Legendary Tanker That Refused to Die* (Annapolis, MD: Naval Institute Press, 2004); Max Hastings [Operation Pedestal] and Sam Moses, *At All Costs: How a Crippled Ship and Two American Merchant Mariners Turned the Tide of World War II* (New York: Random House, 2007).

132 **reframing them as a challenge:** The OptimalWork podcast #168 on "The True Value of Reframing" is very helpful here.

133 **Fred went to sea by himself:** Details about Fred Larsen's life are from the superb 2007 book by Sam Moses, *At All Costs.*

134 **Courage has four:** Aquinas says that Courage, properly speaking, is for facing danger of death, while the four allied virtues are for lesser challenges. Aquinas, *Summa Theologica* II-II, q. 128.

135 **Studies on loss aversion:** S. Gächter, E. J. Johnson, and A. Herrmann, "Individual-Level Loss Aversion in Riskless and Risky Choices," *Theory Decis* 92 (2022): 599–624, https://link.springer.com/article/10.1007/s11238-021-09839-8. M. Norton, L. Aknin, and E. Dunn, "From Wealth to Well-Being: Spending Money on Others Promotes Happiness," *Science* 319, no. 5870 (2008): 1687–1688, https://pubmed.ncbi.nlm.nih.gov/18356530/.

135 **Other research on giving money and social support:** L. Anik et al., *Feeling Good about Giving: The Benefits (and Costs) of Self-Interested Charitable Behavior* (Harvard Business School Working Paper 10-012, 2009), https://doi.org/10.2139/ssrn.1444831.

135 **Still other research:** E. B. Raposa, H. B. Laws, and E. B. Ansell, "Prosocial Behavior Mitigates the Negative Effects of Stress in Everyday Life," *Clinical Psychological Science* 4, no. 4 (2016): 691–698, https://doi.org/10.1177/2167702615611073.

136 **Donating the same amount repeatedly:** E. O'Brien and S. Kassirer, "People Are Slow to Adapt to the Warm Glow of Giving," *Psychological Science* 30, no. 2 (2019): 193–204, https://doi.org/10.1177/0956797618814145.

136 **Research on cancer patients suggests:** H. Xuewei, "Introduction of Magnanimous Psychotherapy," *Universal Journal of Psychology* 6, no. 3 (2018): 80–86, https://doi.org/10.13189/ujp.2018.060302; X. Huang et al., "Effects of Magnanimous Therapy on Coping, Adjustment, and Living Function in Advanced Lung Cancer," *Current Oncology* 26, no. 1 (2019): 48–56, https://doi.org/10.3747/co.26.4126; X. Huang et al., "Effects of Magnanimous Therapy on Emotional, Psychosomatic and Immune Functions of Lung Cancer Patients," *Journal of Health Psychology* 26, no. 7 (2021): 1096–1108, https://doi.org/10.1177/1359105319901312; H. Tao, H. Shen, and D. Wang, "Psychological Effects of Individual Computer Games and

Story-Version Magnanimous-Relaxing Therapy in Patients with Rectal Cancer Surgery," *World Chinese Journal of Digestology* 29, no. 5 (2021): 256–264, https://doi.org/10.11569/wcjd.v29.i5.256.

137 **Also known as *Grit*:** Duckworth, *Grit*. Duckworth's definition of *Grit* actually includes both Perseverance and Resilience. I keep the two separated, following Aquinas, which is more specific in identifying exactly what you're trying to develop.

137 **Individuals who possess a high degree of Perseverance:** A. L. Duckworth et al., "Deliberate Practice Spells Success," *Social Psychological and Personality Science* 2, no. 2 (2011): 174–181, https://doi.org/10.1177/1948550610385872.

137 **Individuals who practice Perseverance and have a positive outlook:** N. H. Zainal and M. G. Newman, "Relation between Cognitive and Behavioral Strategies and Future Change in Common Mental Health Problems across 18 Years," *Journal of Abnormal Psychology* 128, no. 4 (2019): 295–304, https://doi.org/10.1037/abn0000428.

137 **Individuals who consistently have a positive outlook:** C.S. Dweck, "The Journey to Children's Mindsets — and Beyond," *Child Development Perspectives* 11, no. 2 (June 2017): 139–144, https://doi.org/10.1111/cdep.12225.

137 **Research indicates that Perseverance can be improved:** Duckworth, *Grit*.

137 **"Once you quit something, then you can quit something else":** Donald Rumsfeld, *Rumsfeld's Rules: Leadership Lessons in Business, Politics, War, and Life* (New York: HarperCollins, 2013), 1928.

137 **One study on Resilience and high-strain work environments:** A. Shatté et al., "The Positive Effect of Resilience on Stress and Business Outcomes in Difficult Work Environments," *Journal of Occupational & Environmental Medicine* 59, no. 2 (February 2017): 135–140, https://doi.org/10.1097/jom.0000000000000914.

137–138 **Another study found that increased Resilience:** C. Ruini et al., "Well-Being Therapy in School Settings: A Pilot Study,"

Psychotherapy and Psychosomatics 75, no. 6 (2006): 331–336, https://doi.org/10.1159/000095438.

138 **Resilience correlates with increased activation in the prefrontal cortex:** J. A. Rosenkranz, H. Moore, and A. A. Grace, "The Prefrontal Cortex Regulates Lateral Amygdala Neuronal Plasticity and Responses to Previously Conditioned Stimuli," *Journal of Neuroscience* 23, no. 35 (2003): 11054–11064, https://doi.org/10.1523/jneurosci.23-35-11054.2003.

138 **Studies also show that Resilience can be increased:** Shatté et al., "Positive Effect of Resilience"; S. A. Kilic, D. S. Dorstyn, and N. G. Guiver, "Examining Factors That Contribute to the Process of Resilience following Spinal Cord Injury," *Spinal Cord* 51, no. 7 (2013): 553–557, https://doi.org/10.1038/sc.2013.25.

138 **A randomized-controlled trial of a Resilience training approach:** B. G. Bradshaw et al., "Determining the Efficacy of a Resiliency Training Approach in Adults with Type 2 Diabetes," *Diabetes Educator* 33, no. 4 (2007): 650–659, https://doi.org/10.1177/0145721707303809.

138 **"to bring the *Ohio* in at all costs":** Moses, *At All Costs*, 252.

139 **"By now there was mostly dive-bombers comin' in":** Moses, *At All Costs*, 266.

139 **"for heroism above and beyond the call of duty":** Moses, *At All Costs*, 291.

139 **As the subject of his remarks, he chose Courage:** Moses, *At All Costs*, 292.

140 **After Fred died, Minda lived for another twenty-six years:** "Minda Larsen," Dignity Memorial, accessed July 12, 2024, https://www.dignitymemorial.com/obituaries/westwood-nj/minda-larsen-10053656.

140 ***Optimal Work* podcast #193:** Optimalwork.com; there's also a good summary of this at "From Anxiety to Adventure: Kevin Majeres on Reframing Challenges," The Heights Forum, July 14, 2022, accessed

May 1, 2024, https://heightsforum.org/podcast/
from-anxiety-to-adventure-kevin-majeres-on-reframing-anxiety/.

141 **Dr. Mary Steinhart at the University of Texas has developed a
program:** Details on the program are here: "Tranforming Lives
through Resilience Education," The University of Texas at Austin
Kinesiology and Health Education College of Education, accessed
July 12, 2024, https://sites.edb.utexas.edu/resilienceeducation/; M.
Steinhardt and C. Dolbier, "Evaluation of a Resilience Intervention
to Enhance Coping Strategies and Protective Factors and Decrease
Symptomatology," *Journal of American College Health* 56, no. 4
(2008): 445–453, https://doi.org/10.3200/jach.56.44.445-454.

141 **as described by Jia Jiang:** See Andrew Lloyd, "Want to Stop Feeling
Hurt When Someone Says No? Take the Rejection Therapy
Challenge," *Guardian*, July 24, 2022, https://www.theguardian.com/
lifeandstyle/2022/jul/24/if-you-are-hurt-by-rejection-then-take-
the-rejection-therapy-challenge; and Jia Jiang, *Rejection Proof: How I
Beat Fear and Became Invincible through 100 Days of Rejection* (New
York: Harmony Books, 2015). His TED talk is here: Jia Jiang, "What
I Learned from 100 Days of Rejection," TED, May 2015, https://
www.ted.com/talks/jia_jiang_what_i_learned_from_100_days_
of_rejection?language=en. Jia's approach is based on a game
developed by James Conley.

CHAPTER 12: PRACTICAL WISDOM

145 **On a cold January afternoon in 2009:** *Aircraft Accident Report: Loss
of Thrust in Both Engines after Encountering a Flock of Birds and
Ditching on the Hudson River*, National Transportation Safety Board,
May 4, 2010, https://www.ntsb.gov/investigations/accidentreports/
reports/aar1003.pdf, 7.

145 **Practical Wisdom is the superhabit of making and implementing
wise decisions:** I have tried here to show how Practical Wisdom/
Prudence differs from conventional "decision-making." I feel that I have
only scratched the surface, and I recommend strongly that the reader
interested in learning more read Pieper, *The Four Cardinal Virtues*; Fr.
Gregory Pine, O.P., *Prudence: Choose Confidently, Live Boldly*

(Huntington, IN: Our Sunday Visitor, 2022); and Andrew Yuengert, *Approximating Prudence* (New York: Palgrave Macmillan, 2012).

145 Practical Wisdom recognizes that a decision is not properly made until it is implemented: According to Josef Pieper, *prudentia* is "knowledge of reality," which is then "transformed" into a wise decision, and "takes effect directly in its execution." *The Four Cardinal Virtues*, 12.

146 Practical Wisdom … involves a firm grasp of reality: Aquinas, *Summa Theologica* II-II, q. 48, art. 1.

146 many contemporary decision-making processes: Cf., e.g., *7 Steps to Effective Decision Making*, UMass Dartmouth, accessed July 15, 2024, https://www.umassd.edu/media/umassdartmouth/fycm/decision_making_process.pdf; "5 Steps in Decision Making Process," Mometrix Test Preparation, February 1, 2024, https://www.mometrix.com/academy/decision-making-process/#; Kat Boogaard, "This Is How Effective Teams Navigate the Decision-Making Process," *Work Life*, Atlassian, August 15, 2023, https://www.atlassian.com/blog/teamwork/decision-making-process

146 US Airways Flight 1549 departed New York's LaGuardia airport: "thumps and thuds": *Aircraft Accident Report*, 2.

147 Existing data are gathered through the superhabit of Memory: Aquinas, *Summa Theologica* II-II, q. 49, art. 1.

147 There is a complex scientific literature on what exactly memory is: See, e.g., Gregorio Zlotnik and Aaron Vansintjan, "Memory: An Extended Definition," *Frontiers in Psychology* 10 (2019): 2523, doi.org/10.3389/fpsyg.2019.02523.

147 improvements in memory lead to greater mental health and happiness: D. X. Rasmusson et al., "Effects of Three Types of Memory Training in Normal Elderly," *Aging, Neuropsychology, and Cognition* 6, no. 1 (1999): 56–66, https://www.tandfonline.com/doi/abs/10.1076/anec.6.1.56.790; Daniel G. Dillon and Diego A. Pizzagalli, "Mechanisms of Memory Disruption in Depression," *Trends Neurosci.* 41, no. 3 (2018): 137–149, https://www.ncbi.nlm.

nih.gov/pmc/articles/PMC5835184/#:~:text=Compared%20
to%20healthy%20adults%2C%20depressed,)%20%5B4%2C5%5D.

147 **faulty information will lead to faulty decisions:** "For the virtue of
prudence resides in this: that the objective cognition of reality shall
determine action; that the truth of real things shall become
determinative." Pieper, *Four Cardinal Virtues*, 15.

148 **Reflect often on the things you want to remember:** Aquinas,
Summa Theologica II-II, q. 49, art. 1, in *The Summa Theologiae of St.
Thomas Aquinas*, https://www.newadvent.org/summa/3049.
htm#article1.

148 **these four strategies allow you to create a strong mental model:**
See Charles Duhigg, *Smarter Faster Better: The Transformative Power
of Real Productivity* (New York: Random House, 2016), esp. 92–93.

148 **Sully recalled:** Chesley B. Sullenberger and Jeffrey Zaslow, *Highest
Duty: My Search for What Really Matters* (New York: HarperCollins,
2009), 11.

150 **"It was a smooth, continuous descent":** Sullenberger, 149.

150 **I had spent years flying jet airplanes:** Sullenberger, 214.

150 **Judgment:** The Latin word is *intellectus*, commonly translated as
"understanding," defined as "the right estimate about some final
principle." "Judgment" seems to be a better translation. Aquinas,
Summa Theologica II-II, q. 49, art. 2, in *The Summa Theologiae of St.
Thomas Aquinas*, https://www.newadvent.org/summa/3049.
htm#article2.

150 **The operative principles in an air emergency:** Sullenberger, 213.

151 **"It is usually optimal for the first officer to fly":** Sullenberger, 211.

151 **"So he did not pull them":** Sullenberger, 187.

151 **"Not every situation can be foreseen":** Sullenberger, 188.

151 **Even in those early seconds:** Sullenberger, 211.

152 **"My aircraft":** Sullenberger, 331.

152 **"loss of thrust on both engines":** *Aircraft Accident Report*, 2.

152 **Teachability:** Aquinas, *Summa Theologica* II-II, q. 49, art. 3. *Docilitas* is usually translated as "docility," but this word now means "the quality of being quiet and easy to influence, persuade, or control." *Cambridge Dictionary*, s.v. "docility," accessed July 10, 2024, https://dictionary.cambridge.org/us/dictionary/english/docility. This is not at all what *docilitas* means, which is why I prefer "Teachability."

152 **Teachability, by contrast, is an openness to learning:** "A kind of open-mindedness which recognizes the true variety of things and situations to be experienced and does not cage itself in any presumption of deceptive knowledge." It is directly opposed to "a closed mind and know-it-allness," both of which are "fundamentally forms of resistance to the truth of real things." Pieper, *Four Cardinal Virtues*, 16.

152 **Peterson's rule nine:** Peterson, *12 Rules for Life*, 233.

153 **"I had closely studied other airline accidents":** Sullenberger, 39.

153 **In many ways, all my mentors, heroes, and loved ones:** Sullenberger, 15.

154 **"We were too low, too slow":** Sullenberger, 223.

154 **Creativity:** The Latin word here is *solertia*, which means "a keen first estimate or judgment of what should be done," and is usually translated as "shrewdness." Pine, *Prudence*, 81. Like so many other virtue words, *shrewdness* has taken on other meanings, including where *shrewd* has come to mean "given to wily and artful ways or dealing." *Merriam-Webster*, s.v. "shrewd," accessed July 15, 2024, https://www.merriam-webster.com/dictionary/shrewd. Pine suggests "sagacity" as an alternative, and Deferrari has "skill, shrewdness, quickness of mind." But none of these indicates in English that "quick first estimate," and so instead I chose "Creativity" as the translation, because it at least conveys discovery of new information. Pieper speaks of *solertia* as a "nimbleness" serving the "genuine and immutable end of human life." *The Four Virtues*, 17. Creativity certainly conveys nimbleness, and the kind of structured

Creativity described below, when combined with the rest of the virtues, comes as close to *solertia* as anything else.

154 **the right kind of structure actually improves Creativity:** The relationship between structure and Creativity is complex, but the general idea that the right structures can foster Creativity seems to be correct. See, e.g., Lilach Sagiv et al., "Structure and Freedom in Creativity: The Interplay between Externally Imposed Structure and Personal Cognitive Style," *Journal of Organizational Behavior* 31, no. 8 (2010): 1086–1110, https://irp-cdn.multiscreensite.com/ bf4705b1/files/uploaded/Structure%20and%20freedom%20in%20 creativity.pdf.

155 **It was the most physical rush of excitement:** Allen Gannett, *The Creative Curve: How to Develop the Right Idea, at the Right Time* (London: Ebury, 2018).

155 **This appears to be the case with most successful creative work:** Ibid.

155 **"light bulb moment":** "Edison's Lightbulb," The Franklin Institute, accessed July 15, 2024, https://fi.edu/en/science-and-education/ collection/edisons-lightbulb.

156 **Reasoning is the habit of moving logically:** Aquinas, *Summa Theologica* II-II, q. 49, art. 5. I've derived great satisfaction from becoming good at something that's difficult to do well: Sullenberger, 138.

157 **I was judging what I saw out the window:** Sullenberger, 224.

158 **Before I go to work, I build a "mental model":** Sullenberger, 138.

158 **"pay attention to the specific details of a place":** Sullenberger, 193.

158 **"serious rescue effort":** Sullenberger, 225.

158 **he had "noticed there were a lot of maritime resources nearby":** Sullenberger, 226.

159 **"This is the Captain. Brace for impact":** Sullenberger, 336.

159 **"We're gonna be in the Hudson":** Sullenberger, 337.

159 **"No plan survives first contact with the enemy"**: The actual quote is "No plan of operations reaches with any certainty beyond the first encounter with the enemy's main force." "Helmuth von Moltke 1800–91: Prussian Military Commander," Oxford Reference, Oxford University Press, accessed July 15, 2024, https://www.oxfordreference.com/display/10.1093/acref/9780191826719.001.0001/q-oro-ed4-00007547.

159 **"Everyone has a plan until they get punched in the mouth"**: "Mike Tyson Explains One of His Most Famous Quotes," *South Florida Sun Sentinel*, September 28, 2021, https://www.sun-sentinel.com/2012/11/09/mike-tyson-explains-one-of-his-most-famous-quotes-3/.

160 **Preparedness is associated with success in academic and workplace settings:** M. W. Aalbers et al., "Why Should I Prepare? A Mixed Method Study Exploring the Motives of Medical Undergraduate Students to Prepare for Clinical Skills Training Sessions," *BMC Medical Education* 13, no. 27 (2013), https://doi.org/10.1186/1472-6920-13-27; H. Cooper, J. C. Robinson, and E. A. Patall, "Does Homework Improve Academic Achievement? A Synthesis of Research, 1987–2003," *Review of Educational Research* 76, no. 1 (Spring 2006): 1–62, https://doi.org/10.3102/00346543076001001; J. P. Reser and S. A. Morrissey, "The Crucial Role of Psychological Preparedness for Disasters," *InPsych: The Bulletin of the Australian Psychological Society* 31, no. 2 (2009): 14–15; A. W. Suhaimi, "The Importance of Psychological Preparedness among Flood Victims" (paper presented at ISSC 2016 International Conference on Soft Science, Kedah, Malaysia, April 11–13, 2016), https://doi.org/10.15405/epsbs.2016.08.23.

160 **"Every time we push back"**: Sullenberger, 140.

160 **one "wingtip struck the water first"**: Sullenberger, 231.

161 **"Evacuate"**: Sullenberger, 241.

161 **"I can't talk right now"**: Sullenberger, 255.

161 **"Flight 1549 wasn't just a five-minute journey"**: Sullenberger, 16.

161–162 **"I have people coming up to me with tears in their eyes":** Sullenberger, 261.

162 **We usually think of competence and decency … as two separate things:** The argument I'm making here was originally inspired by R. Edward Freeman's critique of what he calls the "separation thesis" in the business world: the idea that "business" and "ethics" can be meaningfully separated. See, e.g., R. Edward Freeman, "Business Ethics at the Millennium," *Business Ethics Quarterly* 10, no. 1 (January 2000): 169–180, https://www.cambridge.org/core/journals/business-ethics-quarterly/article/abs/business-ethics-at-the-millennium/FFA5DF6146BAEDD799D878D0A20FCC3B. The idea was worked out in Andrew Abela and Ryan Shea, "Avoiding the Separation Thesis while Maintaining a Positive/Normative Distinction," *Journal of Business Ethics* 131, no. 1 (September 2015): 31–41, https://www.jstor.org/stable/24703487.

162 **The full definition of a virtue:** Aquinas, *Summa Theologica* I-II, q. 55, art. 4, in *The Summa Theolgiae of St. Thomas Aquinas*, https://www.newadvent.org/summa/2055.htm#article4, substituting "habit" for "quality," as Aquinas recommends.

163 **"virtue signaling":** Verboy, "Virtue Signalling," Urban Dictionary, December 10, 2015, accessed July 15, 2024, https://www.urbandictionary.com/define.php?term=Virtue%20Signalling

CHAPTER 13: JUSTICE

167 **"an easy and creditable way of life":** John Newton, *The Journal of a Slave Trader*, ed. Bernard Martin and Mark Spurrell (London: Epworth, 1962) xiii; cited in William E. Phipps, *Amazing Grace in John Newton* (Macon, GA: Mercer University Press, 2001), 40.

167 **"tearing husbands away":** Jonathan Aitken, *John Newton: From Disgrace to Amazing Grace* (Wheaton, IL: Crossway, 2007), 93.

167–168 **published *Thoughts upon the African Slave Trade*:** Ibid., 319.

168 **Newton "can hardly be criticized":** Ibid., 92. A counterargument here is that during this time, the mid-1700s, other Christian denominations had been criticizing the horrendous practice for a hundred years and more. Quakers began objecting to slavery in the late 1600s, and Catholic popes since at least the early 1400s had issued formal condemnations of it. See, e.g., Eugene IV, bull *Sicut dudum* (January 13, 1435), https://www.papalencyclicals.net/eugene04/eugene04sicut.htm; "Anti-slavery: Raising the Moral Issue," Quakers in the World, accessed July 15, 2024, https://www.quakersintheworld.org/quakers-in-action/57.

168 **Professor Coffey, through careful analysis:** John Coffey, "'I Was an Eye-Witness': John Newton, Anthony Benezet, and the Confession of a Liverpool Slave Trader," *Slavery & Abolition* 44, no. 1 (2023): 181–201, https://doi.org/10.1080/0144039X.2022.2113716; Mark Bridge, "Amazing Grace Author's Slavery Confession Found 'Hidden in Plain Sight,'" *History First*, March 15, 2023, accessed April 29, 2024, https://historyfirst.com/amazing-grace-authors-slavery-confession-found-hiding-in-plain-sight/.

169 **"a real piece of work":** Longman Dictionary of Contemporary English Online defined "a (real) piece of work" as "someone who does nasty things or deceives people in order to get what they want," accessed April 30, 2024, https://www.ldoceonline.com/dictionary/be-a-real-piece-of-work.

169 **Peterson's rule six:** Peterson, *12 Rules for Life*, 147.

170 ***commutation*:** *Merriam-Webster*, s.v. "commutation," accessed July 15, 2024, https://www.merriam-webster.com/dictionary/commutation.

170 **"Distributive Justice" is for many-to-one Justice:** Aquinas, *Summa Theologica* II-II, q. 61, art. 1. Aquinas does not have a category for social Justice. Collectively, though, the practice of all the superhabits of Justice combined contributes to a just society.

170 **paying or charging a fair price for what we buy or sell:** There remains extensive debate on what a fair or "just" price is, but I think that Aquinas's view that the price derived from fair bargaining is the just price, i.e., the market price in the absence of coercion or deception. Aquinas, *Summa Theologica* II-II, q. 77, art. 4. See Daryl Koehn and Barry Wilbratte, "A Defense of a Thomistic Concept of the Just Price," *Business Ethics Quarterly* 22, no. 3 (July 2012): 501–526, https://www.

cambridge.org/core/services/aop-cambridge-core/content/view/
AEFF8681091DFDCA679371BF0D8E6E35/S1052150X00005091a.
pdf/defense_of_a_thomistic_concept_of_the_just_price.pdf.

171 **"surveyor of tides":** Aitken, *John Newton*, 141. The connection with
tides was that incoming ships would have to anchor out until the
tides were favorable for the ship to enter port.

171 **you can never fully repay your mother:** Aquinas, *Summa
Theologica* II-II, q. 80, art. 1.

171 **Honesty:** The virtue of *veritate*, which is a connected virtue of
Justice, is usually translated as "truth." Ibid., II-II, q. 109. I believe
"Honesty" is more easily understandable as a name of a virtue.
Honesty here is not to be confused with *honestas*, which is usually
translated as "Honesty," but refers to one of the integral parts of
Temperance. Ibid., II-II, q. 145.

172 **"and venerated her especially on account of it":** Victor Hugo, *Les
Miserables: A Novel* (Chicago: McDevitt, 1870), 375–376.

172 **There is extensive philosophical debate over whether or not one
should lie in extreme cases:** See, e.g., Tim Mazur, "Lying,"
Markkula Center for Applied Ethics at Santa Clara University,
November 13, 2015, accessed April 30, 2024, https://www.scu.edu/
ethics/ethics-resources/ethical-decision-making/lying/.

173 **improved personal relationships:** Anita E. Kelly and Lijuan
Wang, "A Life without Lies: Can Living More Honestly Improve
Health?" (lecture, APA Annual Convention 2012, Orlando, FL,
August 2–5, 2012).

173 **Neuroscience research suggests that Honesty is a default mode:**
G. Ganis, "Lying and Neuroscience" *The Oxford Handbook of Lying*,
ed. Jörg Meibauer, 455–468 (Oxford: Oxford University Press,
2019), https://doi.org/10.1093/oxfordhb/9780198736578.013.35.

173 **Peterson's rule eight:** Peterson, *12 Rules for Life*, 203.

173 **Swanson had plagiarized most of his rules:** William H. Swanson,
Swanson's Unwritten Rules of Management (Raytheon, 2004); W. J.

King and James G. Skakoon, *The Unwritten Laws of Engineering* (New York: ASME Press, 2001).

173 **"Shall I teach you what knowledge is?":** Confucius, *Analects*, 2.17.

174 **Extensive research links Gratitude with psychological, social, and physical benefits:** R. A. Emmons and A. Mishra, "Why Gratitude Enhances Well-Being: What We Know, What We Need to Know," in K. M. Sheldon, T. B. Kashdan, and M. F. Steger, eds., *Designing Positive Psychology: Taking Stock and Moving Forward* (Oxford: Oxford University Press, 2011), 248–262, https://doi.org/10.1093/acprof:oso/9780195373585.003.0016.

174 **stronger interpersonal relationships:** A. M. Gordon, "To Have and to Hold: Gratitude Promotes Relationship Maintenance in Intimate Bonds," *Journal of Personality and Social Psychology* 103, no. 2 (2012): 257–274, https://doi.org/10.1037/a0028723.

174 **feelings of joy and pleasure:** A. Valikhani et al., "The Relationship between Dispositional Gratitude and Quality of Life: The Mediating Role of Perceived Stress and Mental Health," *Personality and Individual Differences* 141 (April 2019): 40–46, https://doi.org/10.1016/j.paid.2018.12.014.

174 **Other research suggests:** M. E. P. Seligman et al., "Positive Psychology Progress: Empirical Validation of Interventions," *American Psychologist* 60, no. 5 (2005): 410–421, https://doi.org/10.1037/0003-066X.60.5.410.

174 **One study showed:** M. Ng and W. Wong, "The Differential Effects of Gratitude and Sleep on Psychological Distress in Patients with Chronic Pain," *Journal of Health Psychology* 18, no. 2 (2013): 263–271, https://doi.org/10.1177/1359105312439733.

175 **Peterson's fifth rule:** Peterson, *12 Rules for Life*, 113.

176 **studies suggest that talking to strangers makes us happier:** N. Epley and J. Schroeder, "Mistakenly Seeking Solitude," *Journal of Experimental Psychology: General* 143, no. 5 (2014): 1980–1999, https://doi.org/10.1037/a0037323; G. M. Sandstrom and E. W. Dunn, "Is Efficiency Overrated? Minimal Social Interactions Lead to

Belonging and Positive Affect," *Social Psychological and Personality Science* 5, no. 4 (2014): 437–442, https://doi.org/10.1177/1948550613502990.

176 **Research in social psychology:** K. Otake et al., "Happy People Become Happier through Kindness: A Counting Kindness Intervention," *Journal of Happiness Studies* 7, no. 3 (2006): 361–375, https://doi.org/10.1007/s10902-005-3650-z.

176 **Friendliness is considered an important predictor of stronger relationships:** W. G. Graziano and R. M. Tobin, "Agreeableness," in *Handbook of Individual Differences in Social Behavior*, ed. M. R. Leary and R. H. Hoyle (New York: Guilford Press, 2009), 46–61.

177 **He spent many hours each day and often late at night with Cowper:** Aitken, *John Newton*, 141.

177 **As you practice Generosity, you'll experience improvements in your mood:** See, e.g., L. B. Aknin, E. W. Dunn, and M. I. Norton, "Happiness Runs in a Circular Motion: Evidence for a Positive Feedback Loop between Prosocial Spending and Happiness," *Journal of Happiness Studies* 13, no. 2 (2012): 347–355, https://doi.org/10.1007/s10902-011-9267-5; L. B. Aknin et al., "Prosocial Spending and Well-Being: Cross-Cultural Evidence for a Psychological Universal," *Journal of Personality and Social Psychology* 104, no. 4 (2013): 635–652, https://doi.org/10.1037/a0031578; R. N. Lawton et al., "Does Volunteering Make Us Happier, or Are Happier People More Likely to Volunteer? Addressing the Problem of Reverse Causality When Estimating the Well-Being Impacts of Volunteering," *Journal of Happiness Studies* 22, no. 2 (2021): 599–624, https://doi.org/10.1007/s10902-020-00242-8; and M. Norton, L. Aknin, and E. Dunn, "Spending Money on Others Promotes Happiness," *Science* 319, no. 5870 (April 2008): 1687–1688, https://doi.org/10.1126/science.1150952.

177 **"the impoverished, the bereaved, and the sick":** Aitken, *John Newton*, 135.

177–178 **While he was there, a generous benefactor granted him an annual stipend:** Aitken, *John Newton*, 191.

178 **Compliance, or Obedience:** Although Aquinas does not list the
     virtue of Obedience (which I have called "Compliance") in his
     overview of the potential parts of Justice (*Summa Theologica* II-II, q.
     80, art. 1), he does include it as q. 104.

178 **"learn to obey":** Aitken, *John Newton*, 92.

179 **Research in hospital settings:** M. C. Beach et al., "Do Patients
     Treated with Dignity Report Higher Satisfaction, Adherence, and
     Receipt of Preventive Care?," *Annals of Family Medicine* 3, no. 4
     (2005): 331–338, https://doi.org/10.1370/afm.328; N. W. Dickert
     and N. E. Kass, "Understanding Respect: Learning from Patients,"
     Journal of Medical Ethics 35, no. 7 (2009): 419–423, https://doi.
     org/10.1136/jme.2008.027235.

179 **Other studies show that feeling respected in the workplace:** D.
     LaGree et al., "The Effect of Respect: Respectful Communication at
     Work Drives Resiliency, Engagement, and Job Satisfaction among
     Early Career Employees," *International Journal of Business
     Communication* 60, no. 3 (2021): 844–864, https://doi.
     org/10.1177/23294884211016529.

179 **Similarly, students tend to be more engaged and successful:** A. F.
     Singer and S. Audley, " 'Some Teachers Just Simply Care': Respect in
     Urban Student-Teacher Relationships," *#CritEdPol: Journal of Critical
     Education Policy Studies at Swarthmore College* 2, no. 1 (2017),
     https://doi.org/10.24968/2473-912x.2.1.5.

179 **There is, however, research showing:** E.g., M. Titova and K.
     Sheldon, "Happiness Comes from Trying to Make Others Feel
     Good, Rather than Oneself," *Journal of Positive Psychology* 17, no. 1
     (March 2021): 1–15, https://www.researchgate.net/
     publication/349922479_Happiness_comes_from_trying_to_
     make_others_feel_good_rather_than_oneself.

179 **Research on caring for one's parents:** National Academies of
     Sciences, Engineering, and Medicine, Health and Medicine Division,
     Board on Health Care Services, and Committee on Family
     Caregiving for Older Adults, *Families Caring for an Aging America*
     (Washington, D.C.: National Academies Press, 2016).

179 **Studies also show that serving as a caretaker:** S. R. Beach et al., "Negative and Positive Health Effects of Caring for a Disabled Spouse: Longitudinal Findings from the Caregiver Health Effects Study," *Psychology and Aging* 15, no. 2 (2000): 259–271, https://doi.org/10.1037/0882-7974.15.2.259; A. L. Harmell et al., "A Review of the Psychobiology of Dementia Caregiving: A Focus on Resilience Factors," *Current Psychiatry Reports* 13, no. 3 (2011): 219–224, https://doi.org/10.1007/s11920-011-0187-1.

179 **Supporting one's country is linked to strong social bonds:** M. Morrison, L. Tay, and E. Diener, "Subjective Well-Being and National Satisfaction," *Psychological Science* 22, no. 2 (2011): 166–171, https://doi.org/10.1177/0956797610396224.

180 **Being religious is also linked to increases in optimism:** H. G. Koenig, "Religion, Spirituality, and Health: A Review and Update," *Advances in Mind-Body Medicine* 29, no. 3 (Summer 2015): 19–26, https://pubmed.ncbi.nlm.nih.gov/26026153/. J. A. Ford and T. D. Hill, "Religiosity and Adolescent Substance Use: Evidence from the National Survey on Drug Use and Health," *Substance Use & Misuse* 47, no. 7 (2012): 787–798, https://doi.org/10.3109/10826084.2012.667489.

180 **It is also associated with improvements in cholesterol levels:** S. Ansari et al., "The Impact of Religiosity on Dietary Habits and Physical Activity in Minority Women Participating in the Health Is Power (HIP) Study," *Preventive Medicine Reports* 5 (March 2017): 210–213, https://doi.org/10.1016/j.pmedr.2016.12.012.

180 **Individuals who are religious tend to have stronger interpersonal relationships:** Koenig, "Religion, Spirituality, and Health"; W. J. Strawbridge et al., "Religious Attendance Increases Survival by Improving and Maintaining Good Health Behaviors, Mental Health, and Social Relationships," *Annals of Behavioral Medicine* 23, no. 1 (February 2001): 68–74, https://doi.org/10.1207/s15324796abm2301_10.

180 **being religious is a predictor of life satisfaction:** D. Villani et al., "The Role of Spirituality and Religiosity in Subjective Well-Being of

Individuals with Different Religious Status," *Frontiers in Psychology* 10 (2019), https://doi.org/10.3389/fpsyg.2019.01525.

180 **Studies suggest that one can become more religious:** Y. Hsiao et al., "The Effects of a Spiritual Learning Program on Improving Spiritual Health and Clinical Practice Stress among Nursing Students," *Journal of Nursing Research* 20, no. 4 (December 2012): 281–290, https://doi.org/10.1097/jnr.0b013e318273642f; A. Ayten and S. Karagöz, "Religiosity, Spirituality, Forgiveness, Religious Coping as Predictors of Life Satisfaction and Generalized Anxiety: A Quantitative Study on Turkish Muslim University Students," *Spiritual Psychology and Counseling* 6, no. 1 (2021): 47–58, https://doi.org/10.37898/spc.2021.6.1.130.

180 **Ross Douthat's excellent *New York Times* article:** Ross Douthat, "A Guide to Finding Faith," *New York Times*, August 14, 2021, https://www.nytimes.com/2021/08/14/opinion/sunday/faith-religion.html.

180 **"most sung, most recorded, and most loved hymn":** Aitken, *John Newton*, 224.

180 **Amazing grace (how sweet the sound):** "Amazing Grace! (How Sweet the Sound)," Hymnary.org, accessed July 15, 2024, https://hymnary.org/text/amazing_grace_how_sweet_the_sound.

181 **Studies also suggest that individuals tend to consider different allocation principles:** J. T. Scott and B. H. Bornstein, "What's Fair in Foul Weather and Fair? Distributive Justice across Different Allocation Contexts and Goods," *Journal of Politics* 71, no. 3 (July 2009): 831–846, https://doi.org/10.1017/s0022381609090744.

181 **Perceptions of Distributive Justice are associate with favorable attitudes:** K. van den Bos, E. A. Lind, and H. A. M. Wilke, "The Psychology of Procedural and Distributive Justice Viewed from the Perspective of Fairness Heuristic Theory," in *Justice in the Workplace: From Theory to Practice*, ed. R. Cropanzano (Mahwah, NJ: Erlbaum, 2001), 49–66.

181 **Distributive Justice is linked to improved mood:** S. Alexander and M. Ruderman, "The Role of Procedural and Distributive Justice

in Organizational Behavior," *Social Justice Research* 1, no. 2 (June 1987): 177–198, https://doi.org/10.1007/bf01048015.

181 On the contrary, when things are considered unfair: Y. Cohen-Charash and P. E. Spector, "The Role of Justice in Organizations: A Meta-analysis," *Organizational Behavior and Human Decision Processes* 86, no. 2 (November 2001): 278–321, https://doi.org/10.1006/obhd.2001.2958.

181 Research in developmental psychology suggests: P. Rochat et al., "Fairness in Distributive Justice by 3- and 5-Year-Olds across Seven Cultures," *Journal of Cross-Cultural Psychology* 40, no. 3 (2009): 416–442, https://doi.org/10.1177/0022022109332844.

181 Distributive Justice can be improved in various settings: X. Pan et al., "The Effects of Organizational Justice on Positive Organizational Behavior: Evidence from a Large-Sample Survey and a Situational Experiment," *Frontiers in Psychology* 8 (2018), https://doi.org/10.3389/fpsyg.2017.02315.

181 Philosophers can, and do, argue vigorously: See, e.g., *Stanford Encyclopedia of Philosophy*, s.v. "Distributive Justice," September 26, 2017, accessed April 30, 2024, https://plato.stanford.edu/entries/justice-distributive/.

182 "was of vital importance in converting": Aitken, *John Newton*, 319.

182 Newton lived to see the fruits of these efforts: Ibid.; Melissa Petruzzello, "John Newton," in *Encyclopaedia Britannica*, accessed July 15, 2024, https://www.britannica.com/biography/John-Newton; "John Newton," PBS, accessed July 15, 2024, https://www.pbs.org/wgbh/aia/part1/1p275.html.

182 Aquinas gives the following example: Aquinas, *Summa Theologica* II-II, q. 120, art. 1, in *The Summa Theologiae of St. Thomas Aquinas*, https://www.newadvent.org/summa/3120.htm#article1.

183 "Break the rules": Pfeffer, *7 Rules of Power*.

183 Matthew Dicks puts it this way: Dicks, *Someday Is Today*, 114.

183 **"Any law that uplifts human personality is just"**: Martin Luther King, Jr., "Letter from a Birmingham Jail," African Studies Center, University of Pennsylvania, https://www.africa.upenn.edu/Articles_Gen/Letter_Birmingham.html.

183 **you must be willing to pay the price for breaking an unjust law:** Ibid.

CONCLUSION

187 **"Queen of Gospel"**: "Hallelujah, Mahalia!," 64 Parishes, March 19, 2018, accessed July 15, 2024, https://64parishes.org/hallelujah-mahalia; https://www.biography.com/musicians/mahalia-jackson.

187 **In 1947, she recorded a version of "Amazing Grace"**: Diana Chandler, "John Newton's Amazing Grace Maintains Eclectic Appeal at 250 Years," *Biblical Recorder*, November 22, 2023, accessed April 29, 2024, https://www.brnow.org/news/john-newtons-amazing-grace-maintains-eclectic-appeal-at-250-years/.

187 **the hymn became the unofficial anthem:** Bridge, "Amazing Grace Author's Slavery Confession"; Amy Tikkanen, "I Have a Dream," in *Encyclopaedia Britannica*, May 30, 2024, accessed July 15, 2024, https://www.britannica.com/topic/I-Have-A-Dream.

187 **"Tell em' about the dream"**: Rachel Chang, "How Mahalia Jackson Sparked Martin Luther King Jr.'s 'I Have a Dream' Speech," Biography, March 29, 2021, https://www.biography.com/musicians/mahalia-jackson-i-have-a-dream-influence.

187 **began to speak off the cuff:** "Read Martin Luther King Jr.'s 'I Have a Dream' Speech in Its Entirety," NPR, January 16, 2023, https://www.npr.org/2010/01/18/122701268/i-have-a-dream-speech-in-its-entirety.

188 **Captain Sullenberger ... observed:** Sullenberger, 153.

189 **The answer given is that we need to collaborate better:** Aaron De Smet et al., "If We're All So Busy, Why Isn't Anything Getting Done?" McKinsey & Company, January 10, 2022, https://www.mckinsey.com/capabilities/people-and-organizational-performance/

our-insights/if-were-all-so-busy-why-isnt-anything-getting-
done?cid=eml-web.

APPENDIX

199 **The superhabits of the intellectual life:** Aquinas, *Summa Theologica* I-II, q. 57, art. 1.

199 **Science.... Art:** Ibid., art. 3.

199 **A recent Pew survey:** "Spirituality among Americans," Pew Research Center, December 7, 2023, https://www.pewresearch.org/religion/2023/12/07/spirituality-among-americans/#:~:text=83%25%20of%20all%20U.S.%20adults,if%20we%20cannot%20see%20it.

199 **all have virtue traditions:** See Dahlsgard, Peterson, and Seligman, "Shared Virtue."

About the Author

DR. ANDREW ABELA IS the founding dean of the Busch School of Business at the Catholic University of America in Washington, D.C. and an affiliate faculty member at Harvard University's Human Flourishing Program. His award-winning, widely cited research on integrity and effectiveness in business has been published in several academic journals and in three books. Dr. Abela speaks to business leaders about cultivating the superhabits of success in themselves and in their organizations.

Prior to his academic career, Dr. Abela was a brand manager at Procter & Gamble, management consultant with McKinsey & Company, and managing director at the Corporate Executive Board.

He holds an MBA from the Institute for Management Development in Switzerland and a Ph.D. from the Darden Business School at the University of Virginia. He and his wife, Kathleen, live in Great Falls, Virginia, and have been blessed with six children and their first grandchild.

If you're enjoying *Superhabits*, try our app by downloading it using this QR code: